Darius, muscular, with broad shoulders and a narrow waist. His skin was a deep, rich ebony with a smooth, even complexion that glows under the city lights. He wasn't the tallest fellow, with short, tightly coiled black hair, often styled in a neat fade that his mother keeps it well-groomed. With dark brown eyes, almost black, Darius had a piercing gaze that could be both intimidating and captivating. His eyes were framed by thick, well-defined eyebrows. The high cheekbones and the strong jawline gave his face a chiseled look.

 stared out the window, the chain-link fence a hazy boundary between his world and the world outside. At 19, most kids on his block were already tangled in the streets, but Darius was different. Autism painted his world in shades of intense focus and hyper-awareness. He found solace in the predictable patterns of his routines, the rhythm of bouncing a basketball in the concrete yard behind his apartment building.

Today, the heat shimmered off the asphalt, distorting the rim into a wavering mirage. Darius dribbled, the ball an extension of himself, a familiar weight in his hands. Suddenly, a glint of light pierced through the haze. It wasn't the harsh Chicago sun – it was a streak of emerald green, pulsing with an otherworldly hum. Before Darius could react, the light engulfed him, wrapping him in a cocoon of tingling energy.

He stumbled back, the basketball clattering to the ground. Fear gave way to awe as his senses went into overdrive. The rhythmic thump of his own heart echoed in his ears, a bass line to the symphony of the city – distant sirens, car horns, the murmur of voices from neighboring apartments. He could see textures he'd never noticed before, the intricate web of cracks in the pavement, the individual blades of grass struggling through the concrete.

Tentatively, he reached out. The world seemed to sharpen, details blooming under his fingertips. He picked up the basketball, the worn leather cool and surprisingly light. A strange energy crackled beneath his skin, coursing through his veins. He tossed the ball with a flick of his wrist, and it sailed impossibly high, a blur against the blue sky. Time seemed to slow, the arc of the ball hanging suspended in the air before it swished through the net, effortlessly.

A grin stretched across Darius' face, a feeling he rarely experienced – pure, unadulterated joy. This wasn't just heightened senses; this was power. He dribbled again, the ball glued to his hand, moving with an impossible grace. He jumped, defying gravity, the chain-link fence a mere suggestion as he soared above the cramped yard. The city sprawled beneath him, a concrete jungle waiting to be explored.

Darius, the autistic kid who found comfort in routine, had been touched by something extraordinary. The streets that once held him captive now beckoned with a thrilling new challenge. He was no longer just Darius – he was something more. A silent guardian, a protector, a kid on the spectrum who could finally see the world in all its chaotic beauty, and maybe, just maybe, change it for the better.

As Darius landed softly back on the ground, the world seemed to pulse with a new vibrancy. The once-familiar sounds of the city now felt like a symphony, each note clear and distinct. He could hear the rustle of leaves in the distant park, the hum of electricity coursing through the power lines, and even the soft whispers of conversations from blocks away.

Determined to understand his newfound abilities, Darius decided to test his limits. He sprinted down the alley, his feet barely touching the ground. The world blurred around him, and within moments, he found himself at the edge of the neighborhood park. The trees swayed gently in the breeze, their leaves shimmering with an ethereal glow.

Darius approached a large oak tree, its bark rough and ancient. He placed his hand on it, feeling the life force within. The tree seemed to respond, its branches rustling as if acknowledging his presence. He closed his eyes, focusing on the energy coursing through him. He could sense the roots stretching deep into the earth, the sap flowing through the trunk, and the leaves reaching for the sky.

Opening his eyes, Darius noticed a group of kids playing basketball on a nearby court. They were laughing and shouting, their movements fluid and carefree. He watched them for a moment, a pang of longing in his chest. He had always been an outsider, watching from the sidelines. But now, things were different.

With a deep breath, Darius walked over to the court. The kids paused, eyeing him curiously. He picked up a stray basketball and dribbled it a few times, feeling the familiar rhythm. Then, with a burst of speed, he dashed towards the hoop, leaping into the air. Time seemed to slow as he soared, the world below him a blur. He dunked the ball with ease, landing gracefully on the ground.

The kids stared in awe, their mouths agape. One of them, a tall boy with a friendly smile, stepped forward. "That was amazing! How did you do that?"

Darius shrugged, a shy smile playing on his lips. "Just a little practice," he said, his voice steady and confident.

The boy grinned. "Wanna join us? We could use someone like you on our team."

For the first time in his life, Darius felt a sense of belonging. He nodded, joining the game with a newfound confidence. As they played, he realized that his abilities were not just a gift, but a responsibility. He could use them to protect and inspire, to make a difference in the lives of those around him.

And so, Darius embraced his new role, a silent guardian of the city. He continued to hone his skills, exploring the limits of his powers. The streets that once seemed so confining now stretched out before him, full of endless possibilities. With each passing day, he grew stronger, more confident, and more determined to make the world a better place.

In the heart of Chicago, amidst the chaos and noise, a new hero was born. And his name was Darius.

As the sun began to set, casting long shadows across the city, Darius felt a new sense of purpose. The sky was a canvas of oranges and purples, the colors blending seamlessly into one another. The air was thick with the scent of summer – a mix of blooming flowers, freshly cut grass, and the distant aroma of street food wafting from nearby vendors.

Darius walked through the park, his senses heightened. He could hear the soft rustle of leaves as a gentle breeze swept through the trees, the distant laughter of children playing, and the rhythmic chirping of crickets beginning their evening symphony. The world around him was alive, every detail sharp and vivid.

He made his way to the edge of the park, where the cityscape unfolded before him. The buildings stood tall and proud, their windows reflecting the last rays of sunlight. The streets below were bustling with activity – cars honking, people chatting, and the occasional bark of a dog. It was a chaotic symphony, but to Darius, it was beautiful.

As he walked, he noticed a small alleyway tucked between two buildings. It was dark and narrow, the kind of place most people would avoid. But something about it drew him in. He stepped into the alley, the cool shade a welcome relief from the heat of the day. The walls were covered in graffiti, vibrant colors and intricate designs telling stories of the city's past.

Darius continued down the alley, his footsteps echoing softly. He could feel the energy of the city coursing through him, a constant hum that resonated with his own heartbeat. As he reached the end of the alley, he found himself in a small courtyard. It was a hidden gem, a quiet oasis amidst the urban jungle. The courtyard was filled with lush greenery – ivy climbing up the walls, flowers blooming in every corner, and a small fountain trickling softly in the center.

He sat on a bench, taking in the serene beauty of the place. The sound of the fountain was soothing, a gentle melody that calmed his mind. He closed his eyes, letting the peace of the moment wash over him. For the first time in a long while, he felt truly at ease.

But his tranquility was short-lived. A sudden noise shattered the silence – the sound of footsteps approaching. Darius opened his eyes, his senses on high alert. He saw a figure emerge from the shadows, a man in his late thirties with a rugged appearance. The man's eyes were sharp, scanning the courtyard with a predatory gaze.

Darius stood up, his muscles tensing. The man noticed him and smirked, a dangerous glint in his eyes. "Well, well, what do we have here?" he said, his voice low and menacing.

Darius didn't respond, his mind racing. He could feel the energy crackling beneath his skin, ready to be unleashed. The man took a step closer, his smirk widening. "You shouldn't be here, kid. This is my territory."

Without warning, the man lunged at Darius, a knife glinting in his hand. But Darius was ready. He moved with lightning speed, dodging the attack and grabbing the man's wrist. The energy surged through him, and with a flick of his wrist, he sent the man flying across the courtyard.

The man hit the ground hard, groaning in pain. Darius stood over him, his eyes blazing with determination. "This city doesn't belong to you," he said, his voice steady and strong. "It belongs to everyone."

The man scrambled to his feet, fear flashing in his eyes. He took one last look at Darius before fleeing into the shadows. Darius watched him go, a sense of triumph swelling in his chest. He had faced his first real challenge and emerged victorious.

As the night settled over the city, Darius knew that his journey was just beginning. There would be more challenges ahead, more battles to fight. But he was ready. With his newfound powers and a heart full of determination, he would protect his city and its people. He was no longer just Darius – he was a guardian, a hero, and a beacon of hope in the darkness.

As the night deepened, the vibrant hues of the sunset gave way to the cool blues and blacks of the Chicago skyline. Darius, a young Black man with a lean frame and intense eyes, stood at the edge of the Lawndale community, a place the locals called the Holy City. This neighborhood, with its rich history and complex tapestry of lives, was both a sanctuary and a battleground.

The Holy City was a place of contrasts. By day, it bustled with the energy of street vendors, children playing on the sidewalks, and the hum of daily life. The air was filled with the aroma of soul food from corner restaurants, the laughter of families, and the rhythmic beats of hip-hop music spilling from open windows. The buildings, though worn and weathered, stood tall with a sense of resilience, their brick facades telling stories of generations past.

By night, the Holy City transformed. The streets, once filled with the warmth of community, became shadowed and tense. Streetlights cast long, eerie shadows, and the distant wail of sirens was a constant reminder of the dangers lurking in the dark. Yet, amidst this, there was a beauty – the way the moonlight reflected off the graffiti-covered walls, turning them into canvases of urban art, the soft glow of neon signs flickering in the distance, and the occasional firefly dancing in the night air.

Darius walked these streets with a newfound   purpose. His dark skin glistened with a sheen of sweat, a testament to the humid summer night. His senses were heightened, every sound and sight amplified. He could hear the distant chatter of a group of teenagers hanging out on a stoop, the soft rustle of leaves in the breeze, and the faint strains of a saxophone playing somewhere in the distance.

He moved with a grace that belied his years, his every step purposeful. The Holy City was his home, and he knew its every nook and cranny. He passed by the old church on the corner, its stained glass windows glowing softly in the moonlight. The church was a beacon of hope for many, a place where the community gathered to find solace and strength.

As he continued down the street, he saw   familiar faces – Mrs. Johnson, the elderly woman who always sat on her porch, watching the world go by; Marcus, the local barber, closing up shop for the night; and a group of kids playing a late-night game of basketball under the flickering streetlight. They all greeted him with nods and smiles, their eyes reflecting a mix of curiosity and respect.

Darius felt a surge of pride. This was his community, his people. And with his newfound abilities, he was determined to protect them. He knew the challenges that lay ahead – the gangs that roamed the streets, the crooked cops who turned a blind eye, and the drug dealers who preyed on the vulnerable. But he also knew that he had the power to make a difference.

As he reached the end of the block, he paused, looking out over the city. The skyline was a jagged silhouette against the night sky, the lights of downtown twinkling like stars. He took a deep breath, feeling the energy of the city coursing through him. The Holy City was a place of struggle and hardship, but it was also a place of hope and resilience.

Darius knew that his journey was just beginning. With each step, he would uncover more about his powers, face new challenges, and grow stronger. But no matter what lay ahead, he was ready. The Holy City was his home, and he would do whatever it took to protect it. He was Darius, a guardian of the night, a beacon of hope in the darkness, and a hero in the making.In the heart of the Holy City, where shadows often concealed more than they revealed, a new threat emerged. His name was Malik "Shade" Thompson, a man whose presence was as dark and foreboding as the night itself. Malik, a former gang leader turned rogue, had always been a figure of fear and respect in the Lawndale community. But now, with powers that rivaled Darius's, he was a force to be reckoned with.

Malik's transformation began one fateful night when he stumbled upon an ancient artifact hidden in the depths of an abandoned warehouse. The artifact, a relic from a forgotten era, pulsed with a dark energy that called to him. Drawn by its power, Malik reached out and touched it, and in that moment, his fate was sealed. The artifact's energy surged through him, imbuing him with abilities that were both terrifying and formidable.

Malik could control and manipulate shadows, bending them to his will. He could cloak himself in darkness, becoming nearly invisible in the night. This ability allowed him to move undetected, striking fear into the hearts of his enemies. He could also create solid constructs from shadows, forming weapons or barriers that were as strong as steel.

Malik had the power to phase through solid objects, making him nearly impossible to capture. He could walk through walls, evade attacks, and escape from any situation with ease. This ability made him a master of stealth and infiltration, able to strike from the shadows and disappear without a trace.

Malik could harness the dark energy within him to unleash powerful blasts of shadowy force. These blasts could knock back opponents, shatter objects, and create devastating shockwaves. The energy also had a corrupting effect, weakening and disorienting those who were struck by it.

The dark energy coursing through Malik's veins granted him superhuman strength and agility. He could leap great distances, move with incredible speed, and overpower even the strongest opponents. His physical prowess made him a formidable adversary in hand-to-hand combat.

Malik had the ability to instill fear in others, amplifying their deepest anxieties and phobias. This power allowed him to control and manipulate those around him, bending them to his will. The mere sight of him could send shivers down the spine of even the bravest individuals.

Malik, now known as Shade, embraced his new powers with a ruthless determination. He saw himself as the true ruler of the Holy City, a dark king who would bring order through fear and domination. His presence cast a long shadow over the community, and his name became synonymous with terror.

Darius, with his newfound abilities, knew that he had to confront Shade. The two were destined to clash, their powers a stark contrast of light and dark. As Darius prepared for the inevitable battle, he understood that defeating Shade would not be easy. But with his unwavering resolve and the support of his community, he was ready to face the darkness head-on.

The stage was set for an epic showdown in the Holy City, a battle that would determine the fate of the neighborhood and its people. Darius, the guardian of light, and Malik, the harbinger of shadows, would soon meet in a confrontation that would test their limits and define their destinies.
Malik's descent into darkness was driven by a complex web of motivations, each thread pulling him deeper into the shadows. Here are the key factors that fueled his turn to evil:

Malik grew up in the Holy City, a place where power dynamics were constantly shifting. As a former gang leader, he was accustomed to wielding influence and control. The discovery of his powers amplified his desire to dominate, seeing them as a means to cement his authority and rule over the community with an iron fist. The allure of absolute power was too tempting to resist.

Malik harbored deep-seated resentment towards those he believed had wronged him. This included rival gangs, corrupt officials, and even members of his own community who had betrayed him. His powers gave him the means to exact revenge, to make those who had crossed him pay dearly. This thirst for vengeance became a driving force, blinding him to any sense of morality.

Malik understood the power of fear. He had seen how it could control and manipulate people, bending them to his will. His ability to induce fear became a tool to maintain his grip on the Holy City. By instilling terror, he ensured that no one would dare challenge his authority, creating an environment where he could operate without opposition.

In Malik's mind, his actions were justified. He believed that the Holy City needed a strong hand to bring order to the chaos. His experiences had taught him that the world was a harsh and unforgiving place, and only the strongest could survive. His powers, in his view, were a gift that enabled him to impose his own brand of justice, however twisted it might be.

Malik's journey into darkness was also marked by a profound sense of isolation. His powers set him apart, making it difficult for him to connect with others. This alienation fueled his bitterness and anger, pushing him further away from any potential redemption. The more he embraced his powers, the more he distanced himself from humanity, seeing himself as a lone wolf in a world of sheep.

The dark energy that flowed through Malik was inherently corrupting. It fed on his negative emotions, amplifying his worst traits and desires. The more he used his powers, the more they twisted his mind, making it easier for him to justify his actions and harder for him to see the harm he was causing. This corruption was a constant presence, whispering in his ear and urging him to embrace the darkness fully.

Malik's motivations were a tangled mix of personal vendettas, a desire for control, and the corrupting influence of his powers. Together, they created a formidable adversary for Darius, one whose path to redemption seemed all but impossible.

As the moon climbed higher in the sky, casting a silvery glow over the Holy City, Darius felt a chill run down his spine. The encounter with Malik, now known as Shade, had left him with a sense of urgency. He knew that the battle for the soul of the Holy City was just beginning, and he needed to be prepared.

Darius returned to his apartment, a modest one-bedroom unit on the third floor of a brick building. The view from his window overlooked the heart of Lawndale, the streets bustling with life even at this late hour. He could see the flickering lights of the corner store, the neon sign of the local diner, and the distant glow of the city skyline. It was a view he had always found comforting, a reminder of the community he was a part of.

Inside, his apartment was a sanctuary of order and routine. The walls were adorned with posters of his favorite basketball players, and his bookshelf was filled with graphic novels and science fiction books. His desk, neatly organized, held his sketchpad and pencils, tools he used to escape into his own world of creativity.

Darius sat at his desk, his mind racing. He picked up a pencil and began to sketch, the lines flowing effortlessly across the paper. He drew the Holy City as he envisioned it – a place of both beauty and danger, where shadows lurked around every corner. He drew himself, standing tall and resolute, a guardian of the night. And then he drew Shade, a figure cloaked in darkness, his eyes glowing with malevolent intent.

As he sketched, Darius thought about Malik's motivations. He understood that Malik's desire for power and control stemmed from a place of pain and resentment. But he also knew that Malik's actions were causing harm to the very community they both called home. Darius was determined to stop him, to protect the people of the Holy City from the darkness that threatened to consume them.

The next day, Darius decided to seek out allies. He knew he couldn't face Shade alone. He reached out to Marcus, the local barber, who was well-connected in the community. Marcus had always been a mentor to Darius, offering advice and support when he needed it most.

"Marcus, I need your help," Darius said as he entered the barbershop. The familiar scent of aftershave and hair products filled the air, and the sound of clippers buzzed in the background.

Marcus looked up from his work, his eyes narrowing with concern. "What's going on, Darius?"

Darius took a deep breath and explained everything – his newfound powers, the encounter with Shade, and the threat that loomed over the Holy City. Marcus listened intently, his expression growing more serious with each word.

"We can't let Malik tear this community apart," Marcus said firmly. "I'll spread the word. We'll gather people who can help. But you need to be careful, Darius. Malik is dangerous."

Darius nodded, grateful for Marcus's support. "I know. But I can't do this alone. We need to stand together."

Over the next few days, Darius and Marcus worked tirelessly to build a network of allies. They reached out to community leaders, local business owners, and even some of the older gang members who had left the life behind. Slowly but surely, they began to form a coalition of people who were willing to stand up against Shade and his reign of terror.

One evening, as Darius was patrolling the streets, he heard a commotion coming from a nearby alley. He rushed towards the sound, his senses on high alert. As he turned the corner, he saw a group of teenagers being harassed by a couple of Malik's henchmen. The thugs were demanding money, their voices filled with menace.

Darius stepped forward, his presence commanding attention. "Leave them alone," he said, his voice steady and strong.

The henchmen turned to face him, their expressions shifting from surprise to anger. "Who do you think you are?" one of them sneered.

Darius didn't flinch. "I'm someone who won't let you hurt these kids."

With a burst of speed, he moved towards the thugs, his movements fluid and precise. He disarmed them with ease, using his enhanced strength and agility to subdue them. The teenagers watched in awe, their fear giving way to admiration.

"Thank you," one of them said, his voice trembling with relief.

Darius nodded, a sense of pride swelling in his chest. "Stay safe," he said, before disappearing into the night.

As he continued his patrol, Darius knew that the battle against Shade was far from over. But with each act of bravery, each person he protected, he felt more confident in his ability to make a difference. The Holy City was his home, and he would do whatever it took to defend it.

The stage was set for an epic confrontation, a clash between light and dark that would determine the fate of the Holy City. Darius, the guardian of the night, and Malik, the harbinger of shadows, were on a collision course. And as the city held its breath, the people of Lawndale looked to Darius with hope, believing that he could be the hero they needed.

As the days turned into weeks, Darius's reputation as a protector of the Holy City grew. The community began to rally around him, inspired by his courage and determination. He continued to patrol the streets, using his powers to thwart Malik's henchmen and protect the innocent. But he knew that the ultimate showdown with Shade was inevitable.

One humid summer night, as Darius was making his rounds, he received a message from Marcus. "Meet me at the old church. It's urgent," the text read. Darius's heart raced as he made his way to the church, the familiar building standing tall against the night sky.

Inside, the church was dimly lit, the stained   glass windows casting colorful patterns on the worn wooden pews. Marcus stood at the front, his expression grave. Beside him was a woman Darius had never seen before. She was tall and slender, with piercing green eyes and an air of quiet strength.

"Darius, this is Dr. Evelyn Carter," Marcus said, introducing the woman. "She's a scientist who specializes in energy manipulation. She might be able to help you understand your powers better."

Dr. Carter stepped forward, extending her hand. "It's a pleasure to meet you, Darius. Marcus has told me a lot about you."

Darius shook her hand, feeling a spark of hope. "Can you really help me?"

Dr. Carter nodded. "I've been studying phenomena like yours for years. With your permission, I'd like to run some tests to see if we can unlock more of your potential."

Over the next few days, Darius worked closely with Dr. Carter. She set up a makeshift lab in the basement of the church, using advanced equipment to analyze his abilities. They discovered that his powers were linked to a unique energy signature, one that resonated with the very fabric of the city.

"You have a connection to the Holy City," Dr. Carter explained. "Your powers are amplified by the energy of this place. The more you understand and harness this energy, the stronger you'll become."

Darius trained tirelessly, honing his skills and pushing his limits. He learned to control his heightened senses, to channel the energy within him, and to use his powers with precision. With Dr. Carter's guidance, he became more confident and capable, ready to face whatever challenges lay ahead.

One evening, as Darius was practicing in the church courtyard, Marcus approached him with a worried expression. "We've got a problem," he said. "Malik's planning something big. He's gathering his forces for a major attack on the community center."

Darius's heart sank. The community center was a vital part of the Holy City, a place where people came together for support and resources. He couldn't let Malik destroy it.

"We need to stop him," Darius said, determination burning in his eyes. "Gather everyone we can. We'll defend the center with everything we've got."

As night fell, Darius and his allies prepared for the impending battle. The community center was fortified, and people took up positions, ready to defend their home. Darius stood at the front, his senses on high alert, scanning the darkness for any sign of Malik and his forces.

The tension was palpable, the air thick with anticipation. And then, from the shadows, Malik emerged. Cloaked in darkness, his eyes glowed with a malevolent light. Behind him, a group of his henchmen advanced, their expressions grim and determined.

"Darius," Malik called out, his voice echoing through the night. "You can't stop me. This city belongs to me."

Darius stepped forward, his stance unwavering. "You're wrong, Malik. The Holy City belongs to its people. And we won't let you take it from us."

With a roar, Malik unleashed a blast of dark energy, the force of it shaking the ground. Darius countered with a surge of his own energy, the two forces colliding in a brilliant display of light and shadow. The battle had begun.

As the two clashed, the community rallied behind Darius, fighting off Malik's henchmen with a fierce determination. The night was filled with the sounds of struggle – the clash of fists, the crackle of energy, and the shouts of defiance.

Darius and Malik fought with everything they had, their powers pushing each other to the limit. The ground beneath them cracked and splintered, the air charged with energy. Darius could feel the weight of the city on his shoulders, the hopes and dreams of its people driving him forward.

In a final, desperate move, Darius channeled all his energy into one powerful blast. The force of it sent Malik sprawling, his dark energy dissipating into the night. Malik lay on the ground, defeated, his eyes filled with a mix of anger and disbelief.

"It's over, Malik," Darius said, his voice steady. "The Holy City will never be yours."

As the dawn broke, casting a golden light over the city, the people of Lawndale emerged from their homes, their faces filled with relief and gratitude. They had stood together, fought together, and won together.

Darius looked out over the Holy City, a sense of pride swelling in his chest. He knew that the battle was far from over, that there would always be challenges to face. But with his powers, his allies, and the strength of his community, he was ready for whatever came next.

The Holy City was his home, and he would protect it with everything he had. He was Darius, the guardian of the night, a beacon of hope in the darkness, and a hero for his people.

The next day, the sun shone brightly over the Holy City, casting a warm glow on the streets that had witnessed the epic battle the night before. Darius, feeling the weight of exhaustion but also a sense of accomplishment, decided to spend the day with his mother, Mrs. Thompson. She was the heart of his world, a woman whose love and strength had guided him through the toughest times.

They started their day with a trip to the local farmer's market. The air was filled with the scent of fresh produce and baked goods, and the sounds of vendors calling out their wares. Mrs. Thompson, a petite woman with a warm smile and a no-nonsense attitude, navigated the stalls with practiced ease.

"Darius, grab those tomatoes," she instructed, pointing to a pile of ripe, red fruit. "And don't just pick the first ones you see. Check for bruises. We don't want any mushy ones."

Darius chuckled, following her lead. "Yes, ma'am. You know, I think you could give those vendors a run for their money with your bargaining skills."

Mrs. Thompson laughed, a musical sound that always made Darius smile. "Boy, you know I don't play when it comes to getting the best for my family. Now, tell me, how's my superhero doing today?"

Darius shrugged, trying to downplay the events of the previous night. "Just another day in the life, Mom. You know, saving the city, fighting off bad guys. The usual."

Mrs. Thompson gave him a knowing look. "Don't you 'just another day' me, Darius. I heard about what happened last night. You were out there risking your life. You need to be careful."

Darius sighed, feeling the weight of her concern. "I know, Mom. But I can't just stand by and do nothing. People need help, and I have the power to make a difference."

She reached out and cupped his face in her hands, her eyes filled with love and worry. "I know you do, baby. And I'm so proud of you. But remember, you're not invincible. You need to take care of yourself too."

Darius nodded, feeling a lump in his throat. "I will, Mom. I promise."

They continued their shopping, the conversation shifting to lighter topics. Mrs. Thompson regaled him with stories of her youth, her eyes twinkling with mischief. "Did I ever tell you about the time I snuck into a jazz club with your Auntie May? We thought we were so grown, but we got caught by the bouncer and had to wash dishes to pay our way out."

Darius laughed, picturing his mother as a rebellious teenager. "I can't imagine you getting into trouble, Mom. You're always so... proper."

Mrs. Thompson raised an eyebrow. "Oh, I had my wild days, trust me. But those days are long gone. Now, I just worry about my superhero son and his crazy adventures."

As they made their way back home, bags full of fresh produce and baked goods, Darius felt a deep sense of gratitude. His mother was his rock, her love and support a constant source of strength. They spent the afternoon cooking together, the kitchen filled with the delicious aroma of homemade stew and cornbread.

"Darius, pass me the paprika," Mrs. Thompson said, stirring the pot with practiced ease. "And don't skimp on it. We need some flavor in this stew."

Darius handed her the spice, grinning. "Yes, Chef. Anything else?"

She smiled, her eyes crinkling at the corners. "Just keep being you, baby. That's all I ever need."

As they sat down to eat, the conversation   turned serious once more. "Darius, I know you're doing important work out there," Mrs. Thompson said, her tone gentle but firm. "But promise me you'll always come back home. This city needs you, but I need you too."

Darius reached across the table and took her hand, his heart full. "I promise, Mom. I'll always come back home."

They ate in companionable silence, the bond between them stronger than ever. In the heart of the Holy City, amidst the chaos and challenges, Darius found solace in his mother's love. It was a love that grounded him, gave him strength, and reminded him of what he was fighting for.

As the sun set, casting a golden glow over their home, Darius knew that no matter what lay ahead, he would face it with courage and determination. With his mother's love as his anchor, he was ready to protect the Holy City and its people, one day at a time.

As night fell over the Holy City, the familiar hum of urban life took on a more sinister tone. The streets, bathed in the pale glow of streetlights, were a labyrinth of shadows and hidden dangers. Darius, clad in dark, practical clothing that allowed him to move swiftly and silently, set out on his nightly patrol. His senses were heightened, every sound and movement amplified in the stillness of the night.

Darius's first stop was a narrow alleyway where he heard the desperate cries of a woman. He sprinted towards the sound, his feet barely making a sound on the pavement. As he turned the corner, he saw a man brandishing a knife, demanding the woman's purse. Without hesitation, Darius intervened. He moved with lightning speed, disarming the mugger and pinning him against the wall.

"Get out of here," Darius said to the woman, his voice calm but authoritative. She nodded, her eyes wide with gratitude, and ran off. Darius turned his attention back to the mugger. "This city doesn't belong to you," he said, his grip tightening. "Stay out of trouble."

Next, Darius made his way to a known drug hotspot, a dilapidated building on the edge of the neighborhood. He could hear the low murmur of voices and the clinking of glass. Peering through a broken window, he saw a group of dealers arguing over a botched transaction. The tension was palpable, and it was clear that violence was imminent.

Darius burst through the door, his presence commanding attention. "This ends now," he declared. The dealers turned, startled, but Darius was already in motion. He disarmed one, knocked another to the ground, and subdued the rest with a series of swift, precise movements. The drugs were confiscated, and the dealers were left tied up for the authorities to find.

As he continued his patrol, Darius noticed a suspicious figure lurking near a parked car. The figure was attempting to break into the vehicle, using a slim jim to unlock the door. Darius approached silently, his footsteps masked by the ambient noise of the city. Just as the thief managed to open the door, Darius grabbed him by the collar and pulled him away.

"Not tonight," Darius said, his voice low and menacing. The thief struggled, but Darius's grip was unyielding. He dragged the would-be car thief to the nearest police station, ensuring that the vehicle and its owner were safe.

The night was far from over. Darius heard raised voices coming from a nearby apartment building. He climbed the fire escape, his movements fluid and silent, and peered into a window. Inside, a heated argument was escalating into physical violence. A man was shouting at a woman, his anger palpable.

Darius tapped on the window, startling the couple. "Is everything okay in there?" he asked, his tone firm but concerned. The man turned, his face contorted with rage, but Darius's presence was enough to defuse the situation. "Let's talk this out," Darius said, climbing through the window. He mediated the dispute, ensuring that the woman was safe and that the man understood the consequences of his actions.

As the night wore on, Darius noticed a plume of smoke rising from an abandoned building. He sprinted towards it, his heart pounding. Flames licked at the windows, and he could hear the crackling of burning wood. Without a second thought, Darius rushed inside, his senses guiding him through the smoke-filled corridors.

He found a group of homeless individuals trapped inside, their escape routes blocked by the fire. "Follow me!" Darius shouted, his voice cutting through the chaos. He led them to safety, using his enhanced strength to clear debris and his heightened senses to navigate the thick smoke. Once outside, he ensured that everyone was accounted for and called the fire department to handle the blaze.

Finally, as dawn approached, Darius encountered a gang confrontation in a deserted parking lot. Two rival groups were squaring off, weapons drawn, ready for a violent clash. Darius stepped between them, his presence a beacon of authority.

"Enough!" he shouted, his voice echoing through the lot. "This isn't the way." He used his powers to disarm the gang members, his movements a blur of speed and precision. "Go home," he said, his tone leaving no room for argument. "This city has seen enough bloodshed."

As the gang members dispersed, Darius felt a sense of accomplishment. The night had been long and grueling, but he had made a difference. The Holy City was a little safer, thanks to his efforts.

As the first light of dawn broke over the horizon, Darius made his way back home. He was exhausted, but his heart was full. He knew that the fight was far from over, but with each night, he grew stronger and more determined. The Holy City was his home, and he would protect it with everything he had.

As the first light of dawn broke over the Holy City, casting a soft, golden hue over the buildings, Darius made his way back home. The streets were quiet, the chaos of the night giving way to a peaceful stillness. He felt the weight of exhaustion in his bones, but also a deep sense of satisfaction. He had made a difference, and that was what mattered.

Back in his apartment, Darius took a moment to catch his breath. The familiar surroundings brought him comfort – the posters on the walls, the neatly organized bookshelf, and the soft hum of the city outside his window. He washed up quickly, the cool water refreshing against his skin, and changed into clean clothes.

As he stepped into the kitchen, the smell of freshly brewed coffee greeted him. His mother, Mrs. Thompson, was already up, her presence a comforting constant in his life. She was a petite woman with a warm smile and eyes that held a world of wisdom. Her hair, streaked with silver, was neatly styled, and she moved with a grace that belied her age.

"Morning, baby," she said, her voice soft and soothing. "Rough night?"

Darius nodded, sinking into a chair at the kitchen table. "You could say that. But we made it through."

Mrs. Thompson placed a steaming cup of coffee in front of him, her eyes filled with concern and pride. "I heard about what you did. You're out there making a real difference, Darius. But you need to take care of yourself too."

Darius took a sip of the coffee, savoring the warmth. "I know, Mom. It's just... there's so much to do. Malik's not going to stop, and neither can I."

She sat down across from him, her expression serious but loving. "I understand that. But remember, you're not alone. You've got people who care about you, who want to help. Don't carry the weight of the world on your shoulders."

Darius smiled, feeling a surge of gratitude. "Thanks, Mom. I don't know what I'd do without you."

Mrs. Thompson reached out and squeezed his hand, her touch reassuring. "You'd do just fine, because you're strong and determined. But it's okay to lean on others sometimes. Now, how about some breakfast? You need to keep your strength up."

They spent the morning together, cooking and talking. The kitchen was filled with the delicious aroma of pancakes and bacon, and the sound of their laughter echoed through the apartment. Mrs. Thompson shared stories from her youth, her eyes twinkling with mischief.

"Did I ever tell you about the time I tried to impress your father by cooking him a fancy dinner?" she said, flipping a pancake with practiced ease. "I ended up burning everything, and we had to order takeout. He still married me, though."

Darius laughed, picturing the scene. "I guess he knew a good thing when he saw it."

Mrs. Thompson smiled, her eyes crinkling at the corners. "He did. And so do I. You're doing amazing things, Darius. Just remember to take care of yourself too."

As the day wore on, Darius felt a renewed sense of purpose. He knew that the fight against Malik was far from over, but with his mother's love and support, he felt ready to face whatever challenges lay ahead. The Holy City was his home, and he would protect it with everything he had.

That night, as darkness fell once more, Darius set out on his patrol. The city was alive with the sounds of nightlife – the distant thump of music, the murmur of conversations, and the occasional honk of a car horn. He moved through the streets with a sense of purpose, his senses on high alert.

Darius's first stop was a small convenience store where he heard the sound of breaking glass. He sprinted towards the noise, his heart pounding. As he approached, he saw a figure inside, rummaging through the cash register. Without hesitation, Darius burst through the door, his presence commanding attention.

"Stop right there," he said, his voice steady and authoritative. The burglar turned, startled, but Darius was already in motion. He disarmed the thief and restrained him, ensuring that the store was safe.

Next, Darius encountered a street fight between two rival groups. The air was thick with tension, and the sound of fists hitting flesh echoed through the night. Darius stepped between the combatants, his presence a calming force.

"Enough!" he shouted, his voice cutting through the chaos. "This isn't the way." He used his powers to separate the fighters, his movements swift and precise. "Go home," he said, his tone leaving no room for argument. "This city has seen enough violence."

As he continued his patrol, Darius noticed a car speeding down the street, its tires screeching. He recognized it as a stolen vehicle and took off in pursuit. Using his enhanced speed and agility, he caught up to the car and managed to disable it, bringing the thief to justice.

Later, Darius saw smoke rising from a residential building. He rushed towards it, his heart racing. Flames were licking at the windows, and he could hear the panicked cries of the residents. Without a second thought, Darius charged into the building, using his powers to navigate the smoke-filled corridors and lead the residents to safety.

As the night wore on, Darius heard a commotion in a nearby park. He found a man attempting to force a young woman into a van. Darius intervened, his presence a beacon of hope. He subdued the kidnapper and ensured the woman's safety, her gratitude a reminder of why he did what he did.

As dawn approached, Darius made his way back home, exhausted but fulfilled. The Holy City was a little safer, thanks to his efforts. He knew that the fight was far from over, but with each night, he grew stronger and more determined.

Back in his apartment, he found his mother waiting for him, her eyes filled with love and concern. "Welcome home, baby," she said, her voice soft and soothing.

Darius smiled, feeling a surge of gratitude. "Thanks, Mom. It's good to be home."

As the first light of dawn broke over the city, Darius knew that no matter what lay ahead, he would face it with courage and determination. With his mother's love as his anchor, he was ready to protect the Holy City and its people, one day at a time.

As the sun dipped below the horizon, casting long shadows over the Holy City, Darius felt a sense of anticipation. Tonight, he wasn't patrolling the streets or fighting crime. Instead, he was spending time with his girlfriend, Maya. Maya was a beacon of light in his life, her presence a soothing balm to the chaos that often surrounded him.

Maya was a striking woman with a warm, infectious smile and eyes that sparkled with intelligence and mischief. Her curly hair framed her face perfectly, and she moved with a grace that always captivated Darius. They had met a few months ago at a community event, and their connection had been instant and electric.

They decided to meet at their favorite spot, a small rooftop garden that overlooked the city. The garden was a hidden gem, a place where they could escape the hustle and bustle of the streets below. As Darius climbed the stairs to the rooftop, he felt a flutter of excitement. Spending time with Maya was always a welcome respite from his nightly duties.

When he reached the top, he found Maya already there, setting up a picnic. She had laid out a blanket and was arranging an assortment of snacks and drinks. The soft glow of fairy lights strung around the garden added a magical touch to the scene.

"Hey, you," Maya said, looking up with a smile that made Darius's heart skip a beat. "I was starting to think you got lost."

Darius chuckled, walking over to her. "Sorry, had to make sure the city was safe before I could relax. You know how it is."

Maya rolled her eyes playfully. "Always the hero. Well, tonight, you're all mine. No crime-fighting allowed."

Darius sat down beside her, feeling a sense of peace wash over him. "I think I can manage that," he said, leaning in to kiss her. Her lips were soft and warm, and for a moment, the world outside faded away.

They spent the evening talking and laughing, the conversation flowing effortlessly. Maya had a way of making Darius feel at ease, her presence a constant source of comfort and joy. They talked about everything – their hopes and dreams, their favorite books and movies, and the little moments that made life special.

"Do you ever get scared?" Maya asked suddenly, her tone serious. "I mean, with everything you do. It must be terrifying sometimes."

Darius paused, considering her question. "Yeah, I do," he admitted. "But I can't let fear stop me. People are counting on me, and I have to be strong for them. And for you."

Maya reached out and took his hand, her touch grounding him. "I worry about you, you know. I don't want anything to happen to you."

Darius squeezed her hand, his heart full. "I know. And I promise I'll be careful. I have too much to live for to take unnecessary risks."

Maya smiled, her eyes shining with love. "Good. Because I kind of like having you around."

They sat in comfortable silence for a while, watching the city lights twinkle below. The rooftop garden was a sanctuary, a place where they could be themselves without the weight of the world pressing down on them.

As the night grew darker, Darius felt a sense of contentment. Being with Maya reminded him of the simple joys in life, the moments that made everything worthwhile. He knew that the fight against Malik and the darkness that threatened the Holy City was far from over, but with Maya by his side, he felt ready to face whatever challenges lay ahead.

"Thank you for tonight," Darius said softly, his voice filled with gratitude. "I needed this."

Maya leaned her head on his shoulder, her presence a comforting warmth. "Anytime, hero. Anytime."

As they sat together, the city spread out before them, Darius felt a renewed sense of purpose. The Holy City was his home, and he would protect it with everything he had. But he also knew that he didn't have to do it alone. With Maya's love and support, he was stronger than ever.

The night was peaceful, the stars twinkling above, and for a moment, all was right in the world. Darius knew that there would be more battles to fight, more challenges to overcome, but with Maya by his side, he felt ready to face them all. Together, they would navigate the darkness and find the light, one day at a time.

The night air was cool and crisp as Darius and Maya strolled down the street, their hands intertwined. The city was alive with the sounds of nightlife – the distant thump of music, the murmur of conversations, and the occasional honk of a car horn. The streetlights cast a warm glow, creating a cozy ambiance that made the evening feel almost magical.

They had just left their favorite café, where they had spent hours talking and laughing, enjoying each other's company. Maya's laughter still echoed in Darius's ears, a sound that always brought him joy. As they walked, Darius felt a sense of peace, a rare moment of normalcy in his otherwise chaotic life.

But that peace was shattered when Darius's heightened senses picked up the sound of a struggle coming from a nearby alley. His heart rate quickened, and he instinctively scanned the area, his eyes narrowing as he spotted a group of men surrounding a lone figure. The situation was escalating quickly, and he knew he had to act.

"Maya, I just remembered I left something important at the café," Darius said, trying to keep his voice steady. "Can you wait here for a minute? I'll be right back."

Maya looked at him, her brow furrowing with concern. "Are you sure? I can come with you."

Darius shook his head, forcing a smile. "No, it's fine. I'll be quick. Just wait here, okay?"

Reluctantly, Maya nodded. "Okay, but hurry back. I don't like standing around alone at night."

Darius gave her a reassuring squeeze on the hand before turning and jogging back towards the café. As soon as he was out of her sight, he veered off into the alley, his senses on high alert. The sounds of the struggle grew louder, and he could see the group of men more clearly now. They were roughing up a young man, their voices filled with menace.

"Hey!" Darius shouted, his voice echoing off the walls of the narrow alley. "Leave him alone!"

The men turned, their expressions shifting from surprise to anger. "Who the hell are you?" one of them snarled.

Darius didn't waste any time. He moved with lightning speed, his enhanced agility allowing him to dodge their attacks and disarm them with ease. He delivered a series of precise blows, incapacitating the attackers one by one. The young man, now free from their grasp, looked at Darius with a mixture of awe and gratitude.

"Thank you," the young man said, his voice trembling. "I don't know what would have happened if you hadn't shown up."

Darius nodded, his eyes scanning the alley to make sure there were no more threats. "Get out of here and stay safe," he said, his tone firm but kind.

As the young man hurried away, Darius took a deep breath, feeling the adrenaline coursing through his veins. He knew he had to get back to Maya before she started to worry. He quickly made his way back to the street, his mind racing with thoughts of how to explain his absence.

When he reached Maya, she was standing where he had left her, her arms crossed and a worried expression on her face. "What took you so long?" she asked, her tone a mix of concern and irritation.

Darius forced a sheepish smile. "Sorry, I couldn't find what I was looking for. But I'm here now."

Maya sighed, her expression softening. "You had me worried, Darius. Don't do that again."

He wrapped his arms around her, pulling her close. "I promise. Let's get you home."

As they continued their walk, Darius couldn't shake the feeling of unease. He knew that his double life was becoming increasingly difficult to manage, but he also knew that he couldn't stop. The Holy City needed him, and he was determined to protect it, no matter the cost.

But for now, he focused on the woman beside him, her presence a comforting reminder of why he fought so hard. With Maya by his side, he felt ready to face whatever challenges lay ahead, one night at a time.

As Darius and Maya continued their walk, the city lights casting a soft glow around them, Maya couldn't shake a nagging feeling. She glanced at Darius, her eyes narrowing as she noticed something off.

"Darius," she said, her voice tinged with suspicion, "why is your shirt on backwards?"

Darius's heart skipped a beat. He glanced down, realizing too late that in his rush to get back to her, he had put his shirt on incorrectly. He tried to think of a quick explanation, but Maya's skeptical gaze told him she wasn't going to let this slide easily.

"Uh, well," he stammered, scratching the back of his neck, "I guess I was in such a hurry to get back to you that I didn't notice."

Maya raised an eyebrow, her expression a mix of amusement and doubt. "Really? You were in such a hurry that you put your shirt on backwards? Come on, Darius, what's really going on?"

Darius sighed, knowing he couldn't keep dodging her questions. He stopped walking and turned to face her, his eyes earnest. "Maya, there's something I need to tell you. It's not easy, but you deserve to know the truth."

Maya crossed her arms, her gaze unwavering. "I'm listening."

Darius took a deep breath, gathering his thoughts. "The reason I was gone so long is because I saw something happening in that alley. A group of guys were attacking someone, and I had to step in and help. That's why my shirt is on backwards – I had to move quickly."

Maya's eyes widened, her skepticism giving way to concern. "You went into an alley to stop an attack? Darius, that's dangerous! Why didn't you call the police?"

Darius shook his head. "There wasn't time. And... there's more. I have these abilities, Maya. I can move faster, I'm stronger, and my senses are heightened. I've been using them to protect the city, to help people who can't help themselves."

Maya stared at him, her expression a mix of shock and disbelief. "Are you serious? You're like... a superhero?"

Darius nodded, his heart pounding. "Yeah, something like that. I didn't want to keep this from you, but I didn't know how to tell you. I didn't want you to worry."

Maya was silent for a moment, processing everything he had said. Finally, she let out a deep breath. "Darius, I don't know what to say. This is a lot to take in."

"I know," Darius said softly, reaching out to take her hand. "But I promise, I'm always careful. And I do it because I want to make a difference, to protect the people I care about. Including you."

Maya looked into his eyes, her expression softening. "I get that. And I appreciate what you're doing. But you have to promise me you'll be careful. I don't want to lose you."

Darius squeezed her hand, his heart swelling with gratitude. "I promise, Maya. I'll always come back to you."

She smiled, a mixture of relief and affection in her eyes. "Okay, hero. Let's get you home and fix that shirt."

They continued their walk, the weight of the conversation hanging between them but also bringing them closer. Darius felt a sense of relief, knowing that he no longer had to keep his secret from Maya. With her by his side, he felt stronger and more determined than ever to protect the Holy City.

As they reached Maya's apartment, she turned to him, her eyes filled with love and concern. "Just promise me one more thing, Darius."

"Anything," he said, his voice earnest.

"Promise me you'll let me help you. You don't have to do this alone."

Darius smiled, feeling a warmth spread through him. "I promise, Maya. We're in this together."

With a final kiss, they said goodnight, and Darius made his way back to his own apartment. The night had been full of revelations, but he felt a renewed sense of purpose. With Maya's love and support, he knew he could face whatever challenges lay ahead.

The Holy City was his home, and he would protect it with everything he had. And now, he had someone to share that journey with, making the fight for justice and peace all the more meaningful.

Meanwhile, on the other side of town, in a dimly lit warehouse on the outskirts of the Holy City, Malik "Shade" Thompson was deep in thought. The warehouse, once a bustling hub of activity, now stood abandoned, its walls covered in graffiti and its windows shattered. It was the perfect hideout for someone like Malik, a place where he could plot his next move without interruption.

Malik paced back and forth, his mind racing with plans and schemes. The recent setbacks at the hands of Darius had only fueled his desire for revenge. He was determined to not only reclaim his dominance over the Holy City but to extend his reach to the entire city of Chicago. The thought of bringing the city to its knees filled him with a dark satisfaction.

In the center of the warehouse, a large table was covered with maps, blueprints, and various pieces of equipment. Malik's henchmen, a group of loyal followers who shared his vision of chaos and control, stood around the table, waiting for his instructions.

"We need to hit them where it hurts," Malik said, his voice low and menacing. "Darius has been a thorn in our side for too long. It's time to show him and the rest of this city what we're capable of."

One of his henchmen, a burly man with a scar running down his cheek, stepped forward. "What do you have in mind, boss?"

Malik's eyes gleamed with a malevolent light. "We're going to target the city's infrastructure. Power grids, water supply, transportation – everything that keeps this city running smoothly. We'll create chaos and confusion, and while they're scrambling to deal with the fallout, we'll strike at the heart of the Holy City."

He pointed to a map of Chicago, his finger tracing the locations of key facilities. "We'll start with the power plants. A few well-placed explosives will take out the grid and plunge the city into darkness. Then we'll move on to the water treatment plants. Contaminate the supply, and the city will be brought to its knees."

The henchmen nodded, their expressions grim and determined. They knew the risks, but they also knew the rewards. Malik's plan was ambitious, but if successful, it would cement their control over the city.

Malik continued, his voice growing more intense. "And while the city is in chaos, we'll launch a coordinated attack on the Holy City. We'll hit the community centers, the schools, the places where people feel safe. We'll show them that nowhere is safe from our reach."

He paused, his eyes scanning the faces of his followers. "This is our moment. We've been pushed to the sidelines for too long. It's time to take back what's ours and show this city who really runs things."

The henchmen cheered, their voices echoing through the warehouse. Malik felt a surge of satisfaction. His plan was in motion, and soon, the city would be his.

As the night wore on, Malik and his followers worked tirelessly, preparing for the attack.

They gathered explosives, mapped out routes, and coordinated their efforts. Malik's mind was a whirlwind of thoughts and strategies, each one more ruthless than the last.

He knew that Darius would try to stop him, but this time, he was ready. The stakes were higher, and the consequences more severe. Malik was determined to win, no matter the cost.

As dawn approached, Malik stood at the edge of the warehouse, looking out over the city. The skyline was a jagged silhouette against the early morning light, a reminder of the power and potential that lay within his grasp.

"This city will be ours," he whispered to himself, a dark smile playing on his lips. "And there's nothing Darius can do to stop it."

With his plan set in motion, Malik felt a sense of exhilaration. The battle for the Holy City and the entire city of Chicago was about to begin, and he was ready to unleash his full fury.

The stage was set for an epic confrontation, a clash between light and dark that would determine the fate of the city. Malik, the harbinger of shadows, was prepared to do whatever it took to achieve his goals. And as the city held its breath, the people of Chicago would soon find themselves caught in the crossfire of a battle that would change everything.

As the first light of dawn began to creep over the horizon, casting a pale glow over the Holy City, Malik "Shade" Thompson stood at the edge of the warehouse, his eyes fixed on the skyline of Chicago. The city, still shrouded in the early morning mist, seemed peaceful and unaware of the chaos that was about to be unleashed. Malik's mind was a whirlwind of dark thoughts and meticulous plans, each one designed to bring the city to its knees.

Inside the warehouse, his henchmen were busy preparing for the attack. The large table in the center of the room was covered with maps, blueprints, and various pieces of equipment. The air was thick with tension and anticipation, the quiet hum of activity punctuated by the occasional clink of metal or the rustle of paper.

Malik turned back to his followers, his eyes gleaming with a malevolent light. "Remember, we strike at dawn," he said, his voice low and commanding. "The power plants first. We need to plunge the city into darkness. Then we move on to the water treatment plants. Contaminate the supply, and the city will be brought to its knees."

His henchmen nodded, their expressions grim and determined. They knew the risks, but they also knew the rewards. Malik's plan was ambitious, but if successful, it would cement their control over the city.

Malik continued, his voice growing more intense. "And while the city is in chaos, we'll launch a coordinated attack on the Holy City. We'll hit the community centers, the schools, the places where people feel safe. We'll show them that nowhere is safe from our reach."

He pointed to a map of Chicago, his finger tracing the locations of key facilities. "We'll start with the power plants. A few well-placed explosives will take out the grid and plunge the city into darkness. Then we'll move on to the water treatment plants. Contaminate the supply, and the city will be brought to its knees."

The henchmen cheered, their voices echoing through the warehouse. Malik felt a surge of satisfaction. His plan was in motion, and soon, the city would be his.

As the night wore on, Malik and his followers worked tirelessly, preparing for the attack. They gathered explosives, mapped out routes, and coordinated their efforts. Malik's mind was a whirlwind of thoughts and strategies, each one more ruthless than the last.

He knew that Darius would try to stop him, but this time, he was ready. The stakes were higher, and the consequences more severe. Malik was determined to win, no matter the cost.

As dawn approached, Malik stood at the edge of the warehouse, looking out over the city. The skyline was a jagged silhouette against the early morning light, a reminder of the power and potential that lay within his grasp.

"This city will be ours," he whispered to himself, a dark smile playing on his lips. "And there's nothing Darius can do to stop it."

With his plan set in motion, Malik felt a sense of exhilaration. The battle for the Holy City and the entire city of Chicago was about to begin, and he was ready to unleash his full fury.

The stage was set for an epic confrontation, a clash between light and dark that would determine the fate of the city. Malik, the harbinger of shadows, was prepared to do whatever it took to achieve his goals. And as the city held its breath, the people of Chicago would soon find themselves caught in the crossfire of a battle that would change everything.

Darius awoke with a start, the early morning light filtering through his window. He had spent the night with Maya, her presence a comforting balm to the chaos that often surrounded him. But now, as he lay in bed, a sense of unease settled over him. He knew that Malik was out there, plotting his next move.

He quickly got dressed, his mind racing with thoughts of how to protect the city. He knew he couldn't do it alone. He needed to gather his allies and prepare for whatever Malik had planned.

As he made his way to the community center, he couldn't shake the feeling that something big was about to happen. The streets were quiet, the city still waking up, but there was an undercurrent of tension in the air.

When he arrived at the community center, he found Marcus and Dr. Evelyn Carter already there, their expressions serious. "We have a problem," Marcus said, his voice low. "Malik's planning something big. We need to be ready."

Darius nodded, his jaw set with determination. "Let's gather everyone we can. We need to protect the city."

As they worked to rally their allies, Darius felt a sense of urgency. The battle for the Holy City and the entire city of Chicago was about to begin, and he knew that the stakes had never been higher.

With Maya's love and support, and the strength of his community behind him, Darius felt ready to face whatever challenges lay ahead. The Holy City was his home, and he would protect it with everything he had.

The stage was set for an epic confrontation, a clash between light and dark that would determine the fate of the city. And as the city held its breath, the people of Chicago would soon find themselves caught in the crossfire of a battle that would change everything.
As the sun set over the Holy City, casting long shadows across the streets, Malik "Shade" Thompson's plan was set into motion. The city, unaware of the impending chaos, went about its

evening routines. Families gathered for dinner, friends met up at local bars, and the hum of urban life continued as usual. But in the shadows, Malik and his henchmen were ready to strike.

At precisely 8:00 PM, a series of coordinated explosions rocked the city's power plants. The blasts were deafening, sending plumes of smoke and fire into the night sky. Within moments, the entire city was plunged into darkness. Streetlights flickered and died, buildings went dark, and the hum of electricity ceased, replaced by the eerie silence of a city without power.

Panic spread quickly. People stumbled through the darkened streets, their faces illuminated by the glow of their cell phones. Traffic lights were out, causing chaos at intersections. Emergency services were overwhelmed with calls, their resources stretched thin.

Darius was with Maya when the lights went out. They were walking back to her apartment, enjoying the cool evening air, when the city was suddenly plunged into darkness. The explosions in the distance sent a chill down his spine, and he knew immediately that this was Malik's doing.

"Maya, I have to go," Darius said urgently, his voice filled with determination. "This is Malik. He's attacking the city."

Maya's eyes widened with fear and concern. "Be careful, Darius. Please."

He kissed her quickly, his heart pounding. "I will. Stay safe."

With that, Darius sprinted towards the source of the explosions, his enhanced senses guiding him through the darkened streets. The city was in chaos, and he could hear the distant wail of sirens and the panicked cries of its residents. His anger grew with each step, a burning rage at the destruction Malik had wrought.

When Darius arrived at the power plant, the scene was one of utter devastation. The once-mighty structures were now twisted and broken, flames licking at the remains. Firefighters were battling the blaze, their faces grim and determined. Darius's heart ached at the sight of the destruction, but he knew he couldn't dwell on it. He had to find Malik and stop him before more damage was done.

He scanned the area, his heightened senses picking up on the faintest sounds and movements. He could hear the distant murmur of voices, the rustle of footsteps. Malik was close, and Darius was determined to confront him.

Darius found Malik standing on a nearby rooftop, his silhouette stark against the glow of the fires below. Malik's eyes gleamed with satisfaction, a dark smile playing on his lips.

"Enjoying the show, Darius?" Malik called out, his voice dripping with malice. "This is just the beginning. The city will fall, and there's nothing you can do to stop it."

Darius's anger flared, his fists clenching at his sides. "You're wrong, Malik. This city won't fall. Not while I'm here to protect it."

Malik laughed, a cold, mocking sound. "You're just one man, Darius. You can't save them all."

Darius's eyes blazed with determination. "Watch me."

With that, he launched himself at Malik, his   movements a blur of speed and precision. The two clashed in a fierce battle, their powers colliding in a dazzling display of light and shadow. Malik's dark energy crackled around him, but Darius's resolve was unyielding.

The rooftop shook with the force of their blows, the air charged with energy. Darius fought with everything he had, his anger fueling his strength. He knew that he couldn't let Malik win, that the fate of the city depended on him.

As the battle raged on, Darius managed to land a powerful blow, sending Malik sprawling. For a moment, Malik lay on the ground, his expression one of shock and rage. But then he smiled, a dark, twisted smile.

"This isn't over, Darius," Malik said, his voice a low growl. "I'll be back. And next time, you won't be so lucky."

With that, Malik disappeared into the shadows, leaving Darius standing on the rooftop, his heart pounding. The city below was still in chaos, but Darius knew that he had to keep fighting. He couldn't let Malik's actions go unanswered.

As dawn broke over the city, the extent of the damage became clear. The power plant was in ruins, and the city was struggling to cope with the blackout. But amidst the chaos, there was a sense of resilience. People were coming together, helping each other through the crisis.

Darius returned to Maya, his heart heavy with the weight of the night's events. She greeted him with a hug, her eyes filled with concern. "Are you okay?" she asked softly.

Darius nodded, his expression grim. "I'll be fine. But Malik... he's not done. We have to be ready for whatever comes next."

Maya squeezed his hand, her love and support a comforting presence. "We'll get through this, Darius. Together."

As the city began to rebuild, Darius knew that the fight was far from over. Malik's attack had left the city stunned and vulnerable, but it had also strengthened Darius's resolve. He was more determined than ever to protect the Holy City and its people, no matter the cost.

The battle between light and dark was just beginning, and Darius was ready to face whatever challenges lay ahead. With Maya by his side and the support of his community, he knew that he could overcome any obstacle. The Holy City was his home, and he would protect it with everything he had.

As the city reeled from the sudden blackout and the chaos that followed, the Chicago Police Department sprang into action. The explosions at the power plants had left the city in darkness, and the emergency services were overwhelmed with calls. The police, already stretched thin, faced the daunting task of restoring order and ensuring the safety of the city's residents.

The police response was swift but chaotic. Officers were dispatched to the power plants to secure the area and assist with the evacuation of any remaining personnel. The scene was one of utter devastation – twisted metal, smoldering debris, and the acrid smell of smoke filled the air. Firefighters battled the blaze, their faces grim and determined, while police officers set up a perimeter to keep onlookers at a safe distance.

Back at police headquarters, Superintendent Larry Snelling was coordinating the response efforts. His voice was calm but authoritative as he issued orders over the radio. "We need all available units to assist with traffic control and public safety. Prioritize hospitals, fire stations, and other critical infrastructure. We can't afford to let this situation spiral out of control."

The city's emergency response plan was activated, and officers from neighboring districts were called in to assist. The streets were filled with the flashing lights of police cruisers and the wail of sirens as officers worked to manage the chaos. Traffic lights were out, causing gridlock at major intersections, and officers were deployed to direct traffic and prevent accidents.

In the Holy City, the police response was particularly crucial. The community, already on edge from the recent events, needed reassurance and support. Officers patrolled the streets, their presence a calming influence amidst the turmoil. They checked on vulnerable residents, assisted with evacuations, and provided updates on the situation.

At the community center, Marcus and Dr. Evelyn Carter were working tirelessly to coordinate relief efforts. They had set up a makeshift command center, where volunteers were distributing food, water, and blankets to those in need. The police were a vital part of this effort, helping to maintain order and ensure that resources were distributed fairly.

Darius, fueled by anger and determination, joined the police in their efforts. His enhanced abilities allowed him to move quickly through the darkened streets, assisting where he was needed most. He helped direct traffic, guided residents to safety, and provided support to the overwhelmed officers.

At one point, he encountered a group of officers struggling to control a panicked crowd outside a hospital. The power outage had caused a surge in emergency cases, and the hospital was at capacity. Darius stepped in, using his presence and authority to calm the crowd and ensure that those in need received the care they required.

Meanwhile, Malik watched the chaos unfold from his hideout, a dark smile playing on his lips. His plan had worked perfectly, and the city was in disarray. But he knew that this was only the beginning. He had more attacks planned, each one designed to further destabilize the city and cement his control.

He gathered his henchmen, their faces lit by the glow of a single, flickering light. "The power plants were just the first step," he said, his voice low and menacing. "Next, we target the water supply. Without clean water, the city will be brought to its knees."

His followers nodded, their expressions grim and determined. They knew the risks, but they also knew the rewards. Malik's plan was ambitious, but if successful, it would cement their control over the city.

Back at police headquarters, Superintendent Snelling was determined to stay ahead of Malik's plans. He knew that the power plant attacks were just the beginning, and he was already working on contingency plans to protect the city's other critical infrastructure.

"We need to be proactive," he said, addressing his officers. "Malik won't stop until he's brought this city to its knees. We need to anticipate his next move and be ready to respond."

The police worked tirelessly, coordinating with other emergency services and community leaders to ensure that the city remained as safe as possible. They set up checkpoints, increased patrols, and worked to restore power to critical areas.

As the night wore on, Darius felt a renewed sense of purpose. The police were doing everything they could, but he knew that his abilities gave him an edge. He was determined to use his powers to protect the city and stop Malik once and for all.

He returned to the community center, where Marcus and Dr. Carter were still hard at work. "We need to be ready for whatever comes next," he said, his voice filled with determination. "Malik won't stop until he's destroyed everything we care about."

Marcus nodded, his expression serious. "We're with you, Darius. Whatever it takes."

Dr. Carter placed a reassuring hand on Darius's shoulder. "We'll get through this. Together."

As dawn approached, the city began to stir, the first rays of sunlight casting a hopeful glow over the darkened streets. Darius knew that the battle was far from over, but with the support of the police, his community, and Maya by his side, he felt ready to face whatever challenges lay ahead.

The Holy City was his home, and he would protect it with everything he had. The fight between light and dark was just beginning, and Darius was determined to emerge victorious.

As the sun began to rise over the Holy City, casting a warm glow over the community center, Darius felt a sense of urgency. The power plant attacks had left the city in chaos, and he knew that Malik was planning something even more devastating. He had spent the night coordinating with the police and community leaders, ensuring that everyone was prepared for whatever came next.

The community center was a hive of activity. Volunteers were distributing food and water, checking on vulnerable residents, and providing updates on the situation. Darius moved through the crowd, his presence a reassuring sight for those who had come to rely on him.

As he made his way to the makeshift command center, he heard a familiar, chilling voice. "Well, well, if it isn't the city's favorite hero."

Darius turned to see Malik "Shade" Thompson standing at the entrance, his dark eyes gleaming with malice. Malik's presence sent a ripple of fear through the crowd, and people instinctively backed away, their eyes wide with apprehension.

Darius's heart pounded in his chest, but he forced himself to remain calm. "What are you doing here, Malik?" he demanded, his voice steady but filled with anger.

Malik smirked, his expression one of smug satisfaction. "Just checking on my handiwork. I have to say, the blackout was quite the success. The city is in chaos, and it's only going to get worse."

Darius clenched his fists, his anger simmering just below the surface. "You're not going to get away with this. The people of this city won't let you destroy everything we've built."

Malik laughed, a cold, mocking sound that sent shivers down Darius's spine. "You really think you can stop me, Darius? You're just one man, and this city is already falling apart. Face it, you've already lost."

Darius took a step forward, his eyes blazing with determination. "I won't let you win, Malik. I'll fight you with everything I have, and I won't stop until you're brought to justice."

Malik's smile widened, his eyes glinting with amusement. "Oh, Darius, always the hero. But tell me, how does it feel to know that you can't protect everyone? How does it feel to know that no matter how hard you try, you'll never be able to save them all?"

Darius felt a pang of doubt, Malik's words hitting him harder than any physical blow. He knew that Malik was trying to get under his skin, to make him question his resolve. But he couldn't let Malik see that he was getting to him.

"I won't let you break me," Darius said, his voice firm. "This city is stronger than you think, and so am I."

Malik's expression darkened, his amusement giving way to anger. "We'll see about that," he said, his voice low and menacing. "But remember, Darius, every time you fail, every time someone gets hurt because you couldn't save them, that's on you."

With that, Malik turned and walked away, his presence leaving a palpable tension in the air. Darius stood there, his heart heavy with the weight of Malik's words. He knew that Malik was trying to undermine his confidence, to make him doubt his ability to protect the city. And for a moment, he felt a flicker of doubt.

But then he looked around at the people in the community center – the volunteers working tirelessly, the residents banding together to support each other, and the police officers standing ready to defend their home. He saw the strength and resilience of the Holy City, and he knew that he couldn't let Malik's words shake him.

Taking a deep breath, Darius turned back to the command center, his resolve stronger than ever. He had a city to protect, and he wouldn't let Malik's taunts distract him from his mission. With the support of his community and the love of Maya, he knew that he could face whatever challenges lay ahead.

The battle between light and dark was far from over, but Darius was ready to fight with everything he had. The Holy City was his home, and he would protect it, no matter the cost. And as the sun rose higher in the sky, casting a hopeful light over the city, Darius felt a renewed sense of purpose. He was not alone in this fight, and together, they would overcome the darkness.

As Darius left the community center, the weight of Malik's words still lingered in his mind. The sun was now fully risen, casting a warm glow over the city that belied the turmoil within. He knew he couldn't let Malik's taunts get to him, but the doubt had been planted. He needed to clear his head and refocus on the task at hand.

He decided to head to a quiet spot by the river, a place where he often went to think. The path was lined with trees, their leaves rustling softly in the breeze. The sound of the water flowing gently over the rocks was soothing, a stark contrast to the chaos of the city. Darius sat on a bench, taking a deep breath and letting the tranquility of the place wash over him.

As he sat there, his phone buzzed. It was a message from Maya: "Thinking of you. Stay strong. We believe in you."

Darius smiled, feeling a surge of warmth. Maya's support was a constant source of strength for him. He knew he couldn't let her down, nor the people of the Holy City who were counting on him.

Just then, his phone buzzed again. This time, it was Marcus. "Darius, we need you back at the community center. There's been another development."

Darius's heart sank. He knew that Malik wouldn't rest until he had caused as much chaos as possible. He quickly made his way back to the community center, his mind racing with thoughts of what could have happened.

When he arrived, the atmosphere was tense. Marcus and Dr. Evelyn Carter were huddled over a map, their faces etched with worry. "What's going on?" Darius asked, his voice steady despite the anxiety gnawing at him.

Marcus looked up, his expression grim. "Malik's targeting the water treatment plants. If he succeeds, the entire city's water supply could be contaminated."

Darius felt a surge of anger. Malik's plan was more insidious than he had imagined. "We need to stop him," he said, his voice filled with determination. "What's the plan?"

BDr. Carter pointed to the map. "We've identified the most likely targets. We need to secure these locations and prevent Malik from carrying out his plan."

Darius nodded, his mind already formulating a strategy. "I'll take the north plant. Marcus, you and your team handle the south. Dr. Carter, coordinate with the police and get as many resources as you can to the east and west plants."

The team sprang into action, their movements swift and coordinated. Darius felt a renewed sense of purpose. He knew that the stakes were higher than ever, but he also knew that he wasn't alone. With the support of his friends and the community, he felt ready to face whatever challenges lay ahead.

As he made his way to the north water treatment plant, Darius's thoughts turned to Malik. He knew that their paths would cross again, and he was determined to be ready. The city was counting on him, and he couldn't afford to fail.

When he arrived at the plant, the scene was eerily quiet. The facility was a sprawling complex of pipes and tanks, the hum of machinery a constant background noise. Darius moved cautiously, his senses on high alert. He knew that Malik's henchmen could be anywhere, and he needed to be prepared for anything.

As he approached the main control room, he heard voices. He crept closer, his heart pounding. Peering through a window, he saw a group of Malik's men tampering with the controls. Darius knew he had to act quickly.

He burst into the room, his presence commanding attention. "Step away from the controls," he ordered, his voice steady and authoritative.

The men turned, their expressions shifting from surprise to anger. "Who do you think you are?" one of them snarled.

Darius didn't waste any time. He moved with lightning speed, disarming the men and subduing them with a series of precise blows. The fight was intense, but Darius's training and enhanced abilities gave him the upper hand. Within moments, the men were incapacitated, and the threat was neutralized.

Darius quickly checked the controls, ensuring that no damage had been done. He breathed a sigh of relief, knowing that he had prevented a major disaster. But he also knew that this was just one battle in a much larger war.

As he secured the facility, his phone buzzed again. It was a message from Marcus: "South plant secured. No sign of Malik. Be careful."

Darius felt a surge of pride. His team was doing their part, and together, they were making a difference. But he also knew that Malik was still out there, plotting his next move.

As he left the plant, the sun was beginning to set, casting a golden glow over the city. Darius felt a renewed sense of determination. The battle between light and dark was far from over, but he was ready to face whatever challenges lay ahead.

With the support of his friends, the love of Maya, and the strength of his community, Darius knew that he could overcome any obstacle. The Holy City was his home, and he would protect it with everything he had. And as the city held its breath, waiting for the next move, Darius stood ready, a beacon of hope in the darkness.

As the police continued their investigation into the devastating explosion at the power station, the city was still reeling from the blackout. Superintendent Larry Snelling and his team were working tirelessly to piece together the events that led to the attack, coordinating with emergency services to restore order and ensure the safety of the city's residents.

The scene at the power station was one of controlled chaos. Firefighters were still battling the remnants of the blaze, their faces grim and determined. Police officers had set up a perimeter, keeping onlookers at a safe distance while they combed through the wreckage for clues. The air was thick with the acrid smell of smoke and burnt metal, a stark reminder of the destruction Malik had wrought.

Superintendent Snelling stood at the center of the activity, his expression one of focused determination. "We need to find out how they managed to breach security," he said, addressing his team. "Check the surveillance footage, interview the staff, and look for any signs of tampering. We can't afford to miss anything."

Meanwhile, on the other side of town, Malik "Shade" Thompson was already putting his next plan into action. The power station attack had been a success, but it was only the beginning. He knew that the police would be preoccupied with the investigation, giving him the perfect opportunity to strike again.

Malik gathered his henchmen in an abandoned warehouse, their faces lit by the dim glow of a single, flickering light. "The power station was just the first step," he said, his voice low and menacing. "Now, we target the water treatment plants. Without clean water, the city will be brought to its knees."

His followers nodded, their expressions grim and determined. They knew the risks, but they also knew the rewards. Malik's plan was ambitious, but if successful, it would cement their control over the city.

At precisely 10:00 PM, a series of coordinated attacks were launched on the city's water treatment plants. Explosions rocked the facilities, sending plumes of smoke and fire into the night sky. The city's water supply was immediately compromised, and panic spread quickly as residents realized the severity of the situation.

Darius was at the community center when the news broke. His heart sank as he heard the reports of the attacks, knowing that Malik was behind it. He quickly gathered his team, their faces etched with determination.

"We need to secure the remaining plants and prevent further damage," Darius said, his voice steady despite the chaos. "Marcus, take your team to the south plant. Dr. Carter, coordinate with the police and get as many resources as you can to the east and west plants. I'll handle the north plant."

As Darius made his way to the north water treatment plant, his mind raced with thoughts of how to stop Malik. The facility was a sprawling complex of pipes and tanks, the hum of machinery a constant background noise. Darius moved cautiously, his senses on high alert.

When he arrived, he found Malik waiting for him, a dark smile playing on his lips. "I knew you'd come," Malik said, his voice dripping with malice. "But you're too late. The damage is already done."

Darius clenched his fists, his anger simmering just below the surface. "This ends now, Malik. You won't get away with this."

Malik laughed, a cold, mocking sound that sent shivers down Darius's spine. "You really think you can stop me, Darius? You're just one man, and this city is already falling apart. Face it, you've already lost."

Darius took a step forward, his eyes blazing with determination. "I won't let you win, Malik. I'll fight you with everything I have, and I won't stop until you're brought to justice."

Malik's smile widened, his eyes glinting with amusement. "Oh, Darius, always the hero. But tell me, how does it feel to know that you can't protect everyone? How does it feel to know that no matter how hard you try, you'll never be able to save them all?"

Darius felt a pang of doubt, Malik's words hitting him harder than any physical blow. He knew that Malik was trying to get under his skin, to make him question his resolve. But he couldn't let Malik see that he was getting to him.

"I won't let you break me," Darius said, his voice firm. "This city is stronger than you think, and so am I."

Malik's expression darkened, his amusement giving way to anger. "We'll see about that," he said, his voice low and menacing. "But remember, Darius, every time you fail, every time someone gets hurt because you couldn't save them, that's on you."

With that, Malik disappeared into the shadows, leaving Darius standing in the wreckage of the water treatment plant, his heart heavy with the weight of Malik's words. He knew that Malik was trying to undermine his confidence, to make him doubt his ability to protect the city. And for a moment, he felt a flicker of doubt.

But then he remembered the people of the Holy City – the volunteers working tirelessly, the residents banding together to support each other, and the police officers standing ready to defend their home. He saw the strength and resilience of the city, and he knew that he couldn't let Malik's words shake him.

Taking a deep breath, Darius turned back to the task at hand. He quickly assessed the damage, coordinating with the emergency services to secure the facility and prevent further contamination. The battle was far from over, but he was ready to face whatever challenges lay ahead.

As dawn approached, the city began to stir, the first rays of sunlight casting a hopeful glow over the darkened streets. The police and emergency services worked tirelessly to restore order and ensure the safety of the city's residents. The water treatment plants were secured, and efforts were underway to restore the water supply.

Darius returned to the community center, his heart heavy but his resolve stronger than ever. He knew that the fight against Malik was far from over, but with the support of his friends, the love of Maya, and the strength of his community, he felt ready to face whatever challenges lay ahead.

The Holy City was his home, and he would protect it with everything he had. The battle between light and dark was just beginning, and Darius was determined to emerge victorious. And as the city held its breath, waiting for the next move, Darius stood ready, a beacon of hope in the darkness.
As the first light of dawn crept over the horizon, casting a pale glow over the city, Malik "Shade" Thompson stood in the shadows of his hideout, a grim smile playing on his lips. The warehouse, once a bustling hub of activity, now stood silent, its walls covered in graffiti and its windows shattered. The air was thick with the scent of smoke and the faint hum of machinery, a stark reminder of the chaos they had unleashed the night before.

Malik's henchmen were gathered around a large table in the center of the room, their faces lit by the dim glow of a single, flickering light. The table was covered with maps, blueprints, and various pieces of equipment, evidence of their meticulous planning. The atmosphere was tense, the air crackling with anticipation.

Malik stepped forward, his presence commanding attention. "Last night was a success," he said, his voice low and menacing. "The power plants are in ruins, and the city's water supply is compromised. But this is only the beginning. We have more work to do."

One of his henchmen, a burly man with a scar running down his cheek, stepped forward. "What's the next move, boss?"

Malik's eyes gleamed with a malevolent light. "We need to keep the pressure on. The city is already on edge, and we need to push them over the brink. Our next target is the transportation system. We'll hit the subway lines and the major highways. Create gridlock, cause panic, and make it impossible for them to move."

The henchmen nodded, their expressions grim and determined. They knew the risks, but they also knew the rewards. Malik's plan was ambitious, but if successful, it would cement their control over the city.

Malik continued, his voice growing more intense. "We'll use explosives to take out key sections of the subway lines. The resulting chaos will cripple the city's transportation network and make it impossible for them to respond effectively. At the same time, we'll set up roadblocks on the major highways, creating gridlock and preventing any escape."

He pointed to a map of the city, his finger tracing the locations of key targets. "We'll start with the central subway station. It's the hub of the entire network, and taking it out will cause maximum disruption. Then we'll move on to the highways, setting up roadblocks at strategic points to create the most chaos."

The henchmen cheered, their voices echoing through the warehouse. Malik felt a surge of satisfaction. His plan was in motion, and soon, the city would be his.

As the morning light grew stronger, Malik and his followers worked tirelessly, preparing for the attack. They gathered explosives, mapped out routes, and coordinated their efforts. Malik's mind was a whirlwind of thoughts and strategies, each one more ruthless than the last.

He knew that Darius would try to stop him, but this time, he was ready. The stakes were higher, and the consequences more severe. Malik was determined to win, no matter the cost.

At precisely 9:00 AM, a series of coordinated explosions rocked the city's central subway station. The blasts were deafening, sending plumes of smoke and fire into the air. The station, once bustling with commuters, was now a scene of chaos and destruction. People screamed and ran for cover, their faces etched with fear and confusion.

Malik watched from a distance, a dark smile playing on his lips. The explosions had gone off without a hitch, and the city's transportation network was in disarray. He knew that the police and emergency services would be overwhelmed, giving him the perfect opportunity to strike again.

Simultaneously, Malik's henchmen set up roadblocks on the major highways, creating gridlock and preventing any escape. The roads were filled with the sound of honking horns and frustrated drivers, their tempers flaring as they realized they were trapped. The city was in chaos, and Malik reveled in the destruction he had caused.

He gathered his henchmen, their faces lit by the glow of the fires burning in the distance. "This is just the beginning," he said, his voice filled with dark satisfaction. "The city is ours for the taking. And there's nothing Darius can do to stop us."

Meanwhile, across town, Darius was at the community center, coordinating with the police and emergency services. The news of the subway explosions and the roadblocks had just come in, and his heart sank as he realized the extent of the damage.

"We need to act fast," Darius said, his voice filled with urgency. "Marcus, take your team and clear the roadblocks. Dr. Carter, coordinate with the police and get as many resources as you can to the subway station. I'll handle the central station."

As he made his way to the subway station, Darius felt a surge of anger and determination. Malik's actions had left the city in chaos, but he knew that he couldn't let that stop him. The people of the Holy City were counting on him, and he was determined to protect them.

When he arrived at the station, the scene was one of utter devastation. The once-bustling hub was now a twisted wreck of metal and concrete, the air thick with smoke and the acrid smell of burning debris. Emergency services were already on the scene, working tirelessly to rescue those trapped in the wreckage.

Darius quickly assessed the situation, his enhanced senses guiding him through the chaos. He moved with lightning speed, helping to clear debris and rescue survivors. His presence was a beacon of hope amidst the destruction, and the people around him drew strength from his determination.

As Darius worked to clear the station, he heard a familiar, chilling voice. "Enjoying the show, Darius?"

He turned to see Malik standing on a nearby platform, his dark eyes gleaming with malice. "This is just the beginning," Malik said, his voice dripping with contempt. "The city will fall, and there's nothing you can do to stop it."

Darius clenched his fists, his anger simmering just below the surface. "You're wrong, Malik. This city won't fall. Not while I'm here to protect it."

Malik laughed, a cold, mocking sound that sent shivers down Darius's spine. "You really think you can stop me, Darius? You're just one man, and this city is already falling apart. Face it, you've already lost."

Darius took a step forward, his eyes blazing with determination. "I won't let you win, Malik. I'll fight you with everything I have, and I won't stop until you're brought to justice."

Malik's smile widened, his eyes glinting with amusement. "Oh, Darius, always the hero. But tell me, how does it feel to know that you can't protect everyone? How does it feel to know that no matter how hard you try, you'll never be able to save them all?"

Darius felt a pang of doubt, Malik's words hitting him harder than any physical blow. He knew that Malik was trying to get under his skin, to make him question his resolve. But he couldn't let Malik see that he was getting to him.

"I won't let you break me," Darius said, his voice firm. "This city is stronger than you think, and so am I."

BMalik's expression darkened, his amusement giving way to anger. "We'll see about that," he said, his voice low and menacing. "But remember, Darius, every time you fail, every time someone gets hurt because you couldn't save them, that's on you."

With that, Malik disappeared into the shadows, leaving Darius standing in the wreckage of the subway station, his heart heavy with the weight of Malik's words. He knew that Malik was trying to undermine his confidence, to make him doubt his ability to protect the city. And for a moment, he felt a flicker of doubt.

But then he remembered the people of the Holy City – the volunteers working tirelessly, the residents banding together to support each other, and the police officers standing ready to defend their home. He saw the strength and resilience of the city, and he knew that he couldn't let Malik's words shake him.

Taking a deep breath, Darius turned back to the task at hand. He quickly assessed the damage, coordinating with the emergency services to secure the facility and prevent further chaos. The battle was far from over, but he was ready to face whatever challenges lay ahead.

As dawn approached, the city began to stir, the first rays of sunlight casting a hopeful glow over the darkened streets. The police and emergency services worked tirelessly to restore order and ensure the safety of the city's residents. The subway lines were secured, and efforts were underway to clear the roadblocks and restore normalcy.

Darius returned to the community center, his heart heavy but his resolve stronger than ever. He knew that the fight against Malik was far from over, but with the support of his friends, the love of Maya, and the strength of his community, he felt ready to face whatever challenges lay ahead.

The Holy City was his home, and he would protect it with everything he had. The battle between light and dark was just beginning, and Darius was determined to emerge victorious. And as the city held its breath, waiting for the next move, Darius stood ready, a beacon of hope in the darkness.

As night fell over the Holy City, the air was thick with tension. The city, still reeling from the chaos of the day, seemed to hold its breath, waiting for the next move. Darius knew that Malik wouldn't rest until he had caused as much destruction as possible. He had spent the day coordinating with the police and emergency services, but now, as darkness enveloped the city, he felt a sense of foreboding.

Darius was patrolling the streets, his senses heightened, when he heard a familiar, chilling voice. "Looking for me, Darius?"

He turned to see Malik "Shade" Thompson standing in the middle of the street, his dark eyes gleaming with malice. The streetlights cast long shadows, and the air seemed to crackle with energy. Darius's heart pounded in his chest, but he forced himself to remain calm.

"This ends tonight, Malik," Darius said, his voice steady. "I'm not letting you hurt anyone else."

Malik laughed, a cold, mocking sound that sent shivers down Darius's spine. "You really think you can stop me? You're just one man, Darius. And tonight, you'll see just how outmatched you are."

Without warning, Malik launched himself at Darius, his movements a blur of speed and shadow. Darius barely had time to react, his enhanced senses allowing him to dodge Malik's initial attack. The two clashed in a violent explosion of energy, their powers colliding in a dazzling display of light and dark.

Malik cloaked himself in darkness, becoming nearly invisible as he moved. He used the shadows to create solid constructs, forming weapons that he wielded with deadly precision.

Malik phased through solid objects, making it nearly impossible for Darius to land a hit. He moved through walls and obstacles with ease, his form flickering like a ghost.

Malik unleashed powerful blasts of dark energy, the force of which sent shockwaves through the air. The energy crackled with malevolence, weakening and disorienting Darius with each hit.

Darius moved with incredible speed and grace, his punches and kicks landing with superhuman force. He leaped great distances, using his agility to evade Malik's attacks.

Darius's senses were razor-sharp, allowing him to anticipate Malik's moves and react with lightning speed. He could hear the faintest sounds and see in the dimmest light, giving him an edge in the dark.

Darius channeled his inner energy, creating protective barriers and unleashing powerful blasts of light. The energy crackled around him, a beacon of hope against Malik's darkness.

The fight was fierce and relentless, the two combatants moving with blinding speed. Malik's shadow constructs clashed with Darius's energy barriers, the impact sending sparks flying. The street around them was torn apart, the ground cracking and splintering under the force of their blows.

Malik phased through a wall, reappearing behind Darius and striking with a shadowy blade. Darius spun around, his enhanced reflexes allowing him to block the attack just in time. He countered with a powerful punch, the force of which sent Malik sprawling.

But Malik was relentless. He unleashed a barrage of dark energy blasts, each one hitting Darius with bone-jarring force. Darius staggered, his vision blurring as the energy sapped his strength. He knew he couldn't keep this up for long.

Malik's eyes gleamed with triumph as he saw Darius falter. "You're weak, Darius," he taunted. "You can't protect them all. You can't even protect yourself."

Darius gritted his teeth, his anger fueling his determination. He channeled his remaining energy, creating a blinding flash of light that momentarily disoriented Malik. Seizing the opportunity, Darius launched himself at Malik, landing a series of powerful blows.

But Malik recovered quickly, his intangibility allowing him to slip through Darius's grasp. He reappeared behind Darius, delivering a devastating blast of dark energy that sent Darius crashing to the ground.

Darius lay on the ground, his body battered and bruised. He knew he couldn't win this fight, not tonight. Summoning the last of his strength, he created a blinding flash of light, using it as a distraction to make his escape.

He staggered to his feet, his vision swimming as he stumbled down the street. He could hear Malik's mocking laughter echoing behind him, but he forced himself to keep moving. He had to get away, to regroup and recover.

As he made his way through the darkened streets, Darius felt a surge of determination. He had lost this battle, but the war was far from over. He would come back stronger, more prepared, and he would stop Malik once and for all.

Darius finally reached the safety of his apartment, collapsing onto the floor. His body ached with pain, but his mind was clear. He knew what he had to do. He would train harder, push his limits, and find a way to counter Malik's powers.

As he lay there, catching his breath, his phone buzzed. It was a message from Maya: "Thinking of you. Stay strong. We believe in you."

Darius smiled, feeling a surge of warmth. With Maya's love and the support of his community, he knew he could face whatever challenges lay ahead. The Holy City was his home, and he would protect it with everything he had.

The battle between light and dark was just beginning, and Darius was determined to emerge victorious. And as the city held its breath, waiting for the next move, Darius stood ready, a beacon of hope in the darkness.

Darius lay on the floor of his apartment, his body aching from the brutal fight with Malik. The room was dimly lit, the soft glow of the streetlights outside casting long shadows on the walls. He could hear the distant sounds of the city – the hum of traffic, the occasional siren – but his mind was focused on the battle he had just endured.

He took a deep breath, wincing as pain shot through his ribs. Every muscle in his body felt like it was on fire, but he knew he couldn't afford to rest for long. Malik's words echoed in his mind, a constant reminder of the threat that still loomed over the city.

With a groan, Darius pushed himself up into a sitting position. He reached for his phone, the screen lighting up with a message from Maya: "Thinking of you. Stay strong. We believe in you."

Darius smiled, feeling a surge of warmth and determination. He couldn't let Malik win. He had to find a way to stop him, to protect the people he cared about. He knew that he couldn't do it alone, but with the support of Maya and his community, he felt ready to face whatever challenges lay ahead.

Darius spent the next few hours strategizing, his mind racing with thoughts of how to counter Malik's powers. He knew that he needed to train harder, to push his limits and find new ways to use his abilities. He also knew that he needed allies – people who could help him in the fight against Malik.

He reached out to Marcus and Dr. Evelyn Carter, explaining the situation and his plan. They agreed to meet at the community center the next morning to discuss their next steps. Darius felt a sense of relief, knowing that he wasn't alone in this fight.

The next morning, Darius met with Marcus and Dr. Carter at the community center. The building was a hive of activity, with volunteers working tirelessly to support the residents affected by the recent attacks. The atmosphere was tense but determined, a reflection of the community's resilience.

"We need to be ready for whatever Malik throws at us next," Darius said, his voice steady. "I need to train harder, to push my limits. And I need your help."

Marcus nodded, his expression serious. "We'll do whatever it takes, Darius. You're not alone in this."

Dr. Carter placed a reassuring hand on   Darius's shoulder. "We'll work together to find new ways to use your abilities. We'll make sure you're ready for the next confrontation."

Over the next few days, Darius trained relentlessly. He pushed his body to its limits, honing his strength and agility. He practiced using his energy manipulation, creating stronger barriers and more powerful blasts of light. Dr. Carter helped him develop new techniques, using her scientific expertise to enhance his abilities.

As Darius trained, the community rallied around him. People came together to support each other, their determination and resilience a source of strength for Darius. Maya was a constant presence, her love and encouragement giving him the motivation he needed to keep going.

One evening, as Darius was taking a break from training, Maya sat beside him, her eyes filled with concern. "You're pushing yourself so hard, Darius. I worry about you."

Darius took her hand, his heart swelling with gratitude. "I have to, Maya. Malik won't stop until he's destroyed everything we care about. I need to be ready."

Maya nodded, her expression softening. "I know. And I believe in you. Just promise me you'll take care of yourself too."

Darius smiled, leaning in to kiss her. "I promise."

As night fell over the Holy City once again, Darius felt a sense of anticipation. He knew that Malik wouldn't rest, that another attack was imminent. He was patrolling the streets, his senses heightened, when he heard a familiar, chilling voice.

"Back for more, Darius?"

He turned to see Malik standing in the middle of the street, his dark eyes gleaming with malice. The streetlights cast long shadows, and the air seemed to crackle with energy. Darius's heart pounded in his chest, but he forced himself to remain calm.

"This ends tonight, Malik," Darius said, his voice steady. "I'm not letting you hurt anyone else."

Malik laughed, a cold, mocking sound that sent shivers down Darius's spine. "You really think you can stop me? You're just one man, Darius. And tonight, you'll see just how outmatched you are."

Without warning, Malik launched himself at Darius, his movements a blur of speed and shadow. Darius barely had time to react, his enhanced senses allowing him to dodge Malik's initial attack. The two clashed in a violent explosion of energy, their powers colliding in a dazzling display of light and dark.

Malik cloaked himself in darkness, becoming nearly invisible as he moved. He used the shadows to create solid constructs, forming weapons that he wielded with deadly precision.

Malik phased through solid objects, making it nearly impossible for Darius to land a hit. He moved through walls and obstacles with ease, his form flickering like a ghost.

Malik unleashed powerful blasts of dark energy, the force of which sent shockwaves through the air. The energy crackled with malevolence, weakening and disorienting Darius with each hit.

Darius moved with incredible speed and grace, his punches and kicks landing with superhuman force. He leaped great distances, using his agility to evade Malik's attacks.

Darius's senses were razor-sharp, allowing him to anticipate Malik's moves and react with lightning speed. He could hear the faintest sounds and see in the dimmest light, giving him an edge in the dark.

Darius channeled his inner energy, creating protective barriers and unleashing powerful blasts of light. The energy crackled around him, a beacon of hope against Malik's darkness.

The fight was fierce and relentless, the two combatants moving with blinding speed. Malik's shadow constructs clashed with Darius's energy barriers, the impact sending sparks flying. The street around them was torn apart, the ground cracking and splintering under the force of their blows.

Malik phased through a wall, reappearing behind Darius and striking with a shadowy blade. Darius spun around, his enhanced reflexes allowing him to block the attack just in time. He countered with a powerful punch, the force of which sent Malik sprawling.

But Malik was relentless. He unleashed a barrage of dark energy blasts, each one hitting Darius with bone-jarring force. Darius staggered, his vision blurring as the energy sapped his strength. He knew he couldn't keep this up for long.

VMalik's eyes gleamed with triumph as he saw Darius falter. "You're weak, Darius," he taunted. "You can't protect them all. You can't even protect yourself."

Darius gritted his teeth, his anger fueling his determination. He channeled his remaining energy, creating a blinding flash of light that momentarily disoriented Malik. Seizing the opportunity, Darius launched himself at Malik, landing a series of powerful blows.

But Malik recovered quickly, his intangibility allowing him to slip through Darius's grasp. He reappeared behind Darius, delivering a devastating blast of dark energy that sent Darius crashing to the ground.

Darius lay on the ground, his body battered and bruised. He knew he couldn't win this fight, not tonight. Summoning the last of his strength, he created a blinding flash of light, using it as a distraction to make his escape.

He staggered to his feet, his vision swimming as he stumbled down the street. He could hear Malik's mocking laughter echoing behind him, but he forced himself to keep moving. He had to get away, to regroup and recover.

As he made his way through the darkened streets, Darius felt a surge of determination. He had lost this battle, but the war was far from over. He would come back stronger, more prepared, and he would stop Malik once and for all.

Darius finally reached the safety of his apartment, collapsing onto the floor. His body ached with pain, but his mind was clear. He knew what he had to do. He would train harder, push his limits, and find a way to counter Malik's powers.

As he lay there, catching his breath, his phone buzzed. It was a message from Maya: "Thinking of you. Stay strong. We believe in you."

Darius smiled, feeling a surge of warmth. With Maya's love and the support of his community, he knew he could face whatever challenges lay ahead. The Holy City was his home, and he would protect it with everything he had.

The battle between light and dark was just beginning, and Darius was determined to emerge victorious. And as the city held its breath, waiting for the next move, Darius stood ready, a beacon of hope in the darkness.

As Darius lay on the floor of his apartment, catching his breath and feeling the pain from his recent battle with Malik, he knew he couldn't afford to rest for long. The city was still in danger, and Malik was out there, plotting his next move. He had to be ready.

Over the next few days, Darius trained relentlessly. He pushed his body to its limits, honing his strength and agility. He practiced using his energy manipulation, creating stronger barriers and more powerful blasts of light. Dr. Evelyn Carter helped him develop new techniques, using her scientific expertise to enhance his abilities. Marcus and the community rallied around him, providing support and encouragement.

One evening, as Darius was patrolling the streets, he felt a familiar sense of foreboding. The air was thick with tension, and he knew that Malik was near. He moved cautiously, his senses on high alert, when he heard a chilling voice.

"Back for more, Darius?"

He turned to see Malik standing in the middle of the street, his dark eyes gleaming with malice. The streetlights cast long shadows, and the air seemed to crackle with energy. Darius's heart pounded in his chest, but he forced himself to remain calm.

"This ends tonight, Malik," Darius said, his voice steady. "I'm not letting you hurt anyone else."

Malik laughed, a cold, mocking sound that sent shivers down Darius's spine. "You really think you can stop me? You're just one man, Darius. And tonight, you'll see just how outmatched you are."

Without warning, Malik launched himself at Darius, his movements a blur of speed and shadow. Darius barely had time to react, his enhanced senses allowing him to dodge Malik's initial attack. The two clashed in a violent explosion of energy, their powers colliding in a dazzling display of light and dark.

Malik cloaked himself in darkness, becoming nearly invisible as he moved. He used the shadows to create solid constructs, forming weapons that he wielded with deadly precision.

Malik phased through solid objects, making it nearly impossible for Darius to land a hit. He moved through walls and obstacles with ease, his form flickering like a ghost.

Malik unleashed powerful blasts of dark energy, the force of which sent shockwaves through the air. The energy crackled with malevolence, weakening and disorienting Darius with each hit.

Darius moved with incredible speed and grace, his punches and kicks landing with superhuman force. He leaped great distances, using his agility to evade Malik's attacks.

Darius's senses were razor-sharp, allowing him to anticipate Malik's moves and react with lightning speed. He could hear the faintest sounds and see in the dimmest light, giving him an edge in the dark.

Darius channeled his inner energy, creating protective barriers and unleashing powerful blasts of light. The energy crackled around him, a beacon of hope against Malik's darkness.

The fight was fierce and relentless, the two combatants moving with blinding speed. Malik's shadow constructs clashed with Darius's energy barriers, the impact sending sparks flying. The street around them was torn apart, the ground cracking and splintering under the force of their blows.

Malik phased through a wall, reappearing behind Darius and striking with a shadowy blade. Darius spun around, his enhanced reflexes allowing him to block the attack just in time. He countered with a powerful punch, the force of which sent Malik sprawling.

But Malik was relentless. He unleashed a barrage of dark energy blasts, each one hitting Darius with bone-jarring force. Darius staggered, his vision blurring as the energy sapped his strength. He knew he couldn't keep this up for long.

Malik's eyes gleamed with triumph as he saw Darius falter. "You're weak, Darius," he taunted. "You can't protect them all. You can't even protect yourself."

Darius gritted his teeth, his anger fueling his determination. He channeled his remaining energy, creating a blinding flash of light that momentarily disoriented Malik. Seizing the opportunity, Darius launched himself at Malik, landing a series of powerful blows.

But Malik recovered quickly, his intangibility allowing him to slip through Darius's grasp. He reappeared behind Darius, delivering a devastating blast of dark energy that sent Darius crashing to the ground.

Darius lay on the ground, his body battered and bruised. He knew he couldn't win this fight, not tonight. Summoning the last of his strength, he created a blinding flash of light, using it as a distraction to make his escape.

He staggered to his feet, his vision swimming as he stumbled down the street. He could hear Malik's mocking laughter echoing behind him, but he forced himself to keep moving. He had to get away, to regroup and recover.

As he made his way through the darkened streets, Darius felt a surge of determination. He had lost this battle, but the war was far from over. He would come back stronger, more prepared, and he would stop Malik once and for all.

Darius finally reached the safety of his apartment, collapsing onto the floor. His body ached with pain, but his mind was clear. He knew what he had to do. He would train harder, push his limits, and find a way to counter Malik's powers.

As he lay there, catching his breath, his phone buzzed. It was a message from Maya: "Thinking of you. Stay strong. We believe in you."

Darius smiled, feeling a surge of warmth. With Maya's love and the support of his community, he knew he could face whatever challenges lay ahead. The Holy City was his home, and he would protect it with everything he had.

The battle between light and dark was just beginning, and Darius was determined to emerge victorious. And as the city held its breath, waiting for the next move, Darius stood ready, a beacon of hope in the darkness.

The next morning, the sun cast a warm glow over the Holy City, bringing a sense of calm after the previous night's chaos. Darius, still feeling the aches and pains from his confrontation with Malik, decided to spend the day with his mother, Mrs. Thompson. He knew that her presence would be a comforting balm to his weary soul.

Mrs. Thompson was a petite woman with a no-nonsense attitude and a heart as big as the city itself. Her eyes, a deep, soulful brown, held a wisdom that came from years of navigating life's challenges. Her hair, streaked with silver, was always neatly styled, and she moved with a grace that belied her age.

They started their day with a trip to the local farmer's market. The air was filled with the scent of fresh produce and baked goods, and the sounds of vendors calling out their wares. Mrs. Thompson navigated the stalls with practiced ease, her sharp eyes scanning for the best deals.

"Darius, grab those tomatoes," she instructed, pointing to a pile of ripe, red fruit. "And don't just pick the first ones you see. Check for bruises. We don't want any mushy ones."

Darius chuckled, following her lead. "Yes, ma'am. You know, I think you could give those vendors a run for their money with your bargaining skills."

Mrs. Thompson laughed, a sound that was both musical and comforting. "Boy, you know I don't play when it comes to getting the best for my family. Now, tell me, how's my superhero doing today?"

Darius shrugged, trying to downplay the events of the previous night. "Just another day in the life, Mom. You know, saving the city, fighting off bad guys. The usual."

Mrs. Thompson gave him a knowing look, her eyes twinkling with a mix of pride and concern. "Don't you 'just another day' me, Darius. I heard about what happened last night. You were out there risking your life. You need to be careful."

Darius sighed, feeling the weight of her concern. "I know, Mom. But I can't just stand by and do nothing. People need help, and I have the power to make a difference."

She reached out and cupped his face in her hands, her touch warm and reassuring. "I know you do, baby. And I'm so proud of you. But remember, you're not invincible. You need to take care of yourself too."

Darius nodded, feeling a lump in his throat. "I will, Mom. I promise."

They continued their shopping, the conversation shifting to lighter topics. Mrs. Thompson regaled him with stories of her youth, her eyes sparkling with mischief. "Did I ever tell you about the time I snuck into a jazz club with your Auntie May? We thought we were so grown, but we got caught by the bouncer and had to wash dishes to pay our way out."

Darius laughed, picturing his mother as a rebellious teenager. "I can't imagine you getting into trouble, Mom. You're always so... proper."

Mrs. Thompson raised an eyebrow, a playful smile on her lips. "Oh, I had my wild days, trust me. But those days are long gone. Now, I just worry about my superhero son and his crazy adventures."

As they made their way back home, bags full of fresh produce and baked goods, Darius felt a deep sense of gratitude. His mother was his rock, her love and support a constant source of strength. They spent the afternoon cooking together, the kitchen filled with the delicious aroma of homemade stew and cornbread.

"Darius, pass me the paprika," Mrs. Thompson said, stirring the pot with practiced ease. "And don't skimp on it. We need some flavor in this stew."

Darius handed her the spice, grinning. "Yes, Chef. Anything else?"

She smiled, her eyes crinkling at the corners. "Just keep being you, baby. That's all I ever need."

As they sat down to eat, the conversation turned serious once more. "Darius, I know you're doing important work out there," Mrs. Thompson said, her tone gentle but firm. "But promise me you'll always come back home. This city needs you, but I need you too."

Darius reached across the table and took her hand, his heart full. "I promise, Mom. I'll always come back home."

They ate in companionable silence, the bond between them stronger than ever. In the heart of the Holy City, amidst the chaos and challenges, Darius found solace in his mother's love. It was a love that grounded him, gave him strength, and reminded him of what he was fighting for.

As the sun set, casting a golden glow over their home, Darius knew that no matter what lay ahead, he would face it with courage and determination. With his mother's love as his anchor, he was ready to protect the Holy City and its people, one day at a time.

As the sun set over the Holy City, casting a warm, golden glow over the streets, Darius's mother, Mrs. Thompson, and his girlfriend, Maya, found themselves in the cozy kitchen of the Thompson household. The aroma of homemade stew and freshly baked cornbread filled the air, creating a comforting atmosphere that contrasted sharply with the chaos outside.

Mrs. Thompson, a petite woman with a no-nonsense attitude and a heart as big as the city itself, moved gracefully around the kitchen, her hands deftly preparing the evening meal. Her eyes, a deep, soulful brown, held a wisdom that came from years of navigating life's challenges. Her hair, streaked with silver, was neatly styled, and she wore a warm, welcoming smile.

Maya, a striking woman with a warm, infectious smile and eyes that sparkled with intelligence and mischief, was helping set the table. Her curly hair framed her face perfectly, and she moved with a grace that always captivated Darius. She had become a beloved member of the Thompson household, her presence a source of joy and comfort.

"Thank you for helping out, Maya," Mrs. Thompson said, her voice filled with warmth. "It's always nice to have an extra pair of hands in the kitchen."

Maya smiled, her eyes twinkling. "It's my pleasure, Mrs. Thompson. I love spending time here. It feels like home."

Mrs. Thompson paused, her expression softening. "You know, Maya, you mean a lot to Darius. He's been through so much, and having you by his side has made all the difference."

Maya's smile widened, a blush creeping up her cheeks. "He means the world to me too. I just want to support him in any way I can."

Mrs. Thompson nodded, her eyes filled with gratitude. "You're a good woman, Maya. And I can see how much you care about him. Just promise me you'll take care of each other. This city needs him, but he needs you too."

Maya reached out and took Mrs. Thompson's hand, her touch gentle and reassuring. "I promise. We'll get through this together."

They continued their preparations, the kitchen filled with the sounds of clinking dishes and soft laughter. The bond between them was strong, a testament to the love and support that had become the foundation of their family.

As they sat down to eat, the conversation turned to lighter topics. Mrs. Thompson regaled Maya with stories of Darius's childhood, her eyes sparkling with mischief.

"Did I ever tell you about the time Darius tried to build a rocket in the backyard? He was convinced he could reach the moon with a few soda bottles and some baking soda."

Maya laughed, picturing a young Darius with his makeshift rocket. "That sounds like him. Always dreaming big."

Mrs. Thompson chuckled, her expression fond. "He's always had a big heart and a strong sense of justice. Even as a child, he wanted to make the world a better place."

Maya's eyes softened, her love for Darius evident. "And he still does. He's out there every night, fighting to protect this city. I'm so proud of him."

Mrs. Thompson reached across the table and squeezed Maya's hand. "We both are. And with you by his side, I know he'll be able to face whatever challenges come his way."

As the evening wore on, the bond between Mrs. Thompson and Maya grew stronger. They shared stories, laughter, and a deep sense of love and support for Darius. In the heart of the Holy City, amidst the chaos and challenges, they found solace in each other's company.

The night was peaceful, the stars twinkling above, and for a moment, all was right in the world. Mrs. Thompson and Maya knew that the fight was far from over, but with their love and support, Darius would be ready to face whatever challenges lay ahead. Together, they would navigate the darkness and find the light, one day at a time.

As the evening deepened, the cozy kitchen of the Thompson household was filled with the warm glow of the overhead light and the comforting aroma of homemade stew and freshly baked cornbread. Mrs. Thompson and Maya sat at the table, their conversation flowing easily as they shared stories and laughter.

Mrs. Thompson, her eyes twinkling with mischief, continued to regale Maya with tales of Darius's childhood. "You know, there was this one time when Darius decided he was going to be a detective. He must have been about eight years old. He made himself a little badge out of cardboard and went around the neighborhood 'solving' mysteries."

Maya laughed, picturing a young Darius with his makeshift detective gear. "That sounds adorable. Did he actually solve any mysteries?"

Mrs. Thompson chuckled, her expression fond. "Well, he did manage to find Mrs. Jenkins's missing cat. Turned out it was just hiding under her porch the whole time. But Darius was so proud of himself. He even wrote up a little report and everything."

Maya's eyes softened, her love for Darius evident. "He's always had that drive to help people, hasn't he?"

Mrs. Thompson nodded, her smile widening. "Yes, he has. Even as a child, he had a big heart and a strong sense of justice. It's no surprise he's out there now, doing everything he can to protect this city."

Maya reached across the table and took Mrs. Thompson's hand, her touch gentle and reassuring. "And he's not alone. We're all here to support him, to make sure he knows he's not fighting this battle by himself."

Mrs. Thompson squeezed Maya's hand, her eyes filled with gratitude. "Thank you, Maya. It means the world to me to know that he has someone like you by his side."

They continued their meal, the conversation shifting to lighter topics. The bond between them grew stronger with each passing moment, a testament to the love and support that had become the foundation of their family.

As they finished dinner, Mrs. Thompson stood up and began clearing the table. "Maya, why don't you go relax in the living room? I'll take care of the dishes."

Maya shook her head, a playful smile on her lips. "No way, Mrs. Thompson. I'm not letting you do all the work. Let me help."

Mrs. Thompson laughed, her eyes crinkling at the corners. "Alright, alright. I won't argue with you. Let's get these dishes done together."

They worked side by side, the sound of running water and clinking dishes filling the kitchen. The atmosphere was one of warmth and camaraderie, a stark contrast to the chaos outside. As they finished up, Mrs. Thompson turned to Maya, her expression serious but loving.

"Maya, I want you to know that you're a part of this family now. And no matter what happens, we'll face it together."

Maya felt a lump in her throat, her eyes misting with emotion. "Thank you, Mrs. Thompson. That means so much to me."

Mrs. Thompson pulled her into a warm embrace, her touch comforting and reassuring. "We're stronger together, Maya. And with you by Darius's side, I know he'll be able to face whatever challenges come his way."

As they moved to the living room, the conversation turned to their hopes and dreams for the future. They talked about the things they wanted to do, the places they wanted to see, and the life they hoped to build together with Darius.

The night was peaceful, the stars twinkling above, and for a moment, all was right in the world. Mrs. Thompson and Maya knew that the fight was far from over, but with their love and support, Darius would be ready to face whatever challenges lay ahead. Together, they would navigate the darkness and find the light, one day at a time.

As the evening drew to a close, Maya received a text from Darius: "Heading home soon. Can't wait to see you."

She smiled, her heart swelling with love and anticipation. "Darius is on his way back," she said to Mrs. Thompson. "He'll be here soon."

Mrs. Thompson nodded, her eyes filled with warmth. "Good. We'll be here waiting for him."

And so, as the night deepened, the Thompson household remained a beacon of hope and love in the heart of the Holy City. With the support of his mother and the love of Maya, Darius knew he could face whatever challenges lay ahead. The battle between light and dark was just beginning, but together, they would find the strength to overcome it.

As the sun dipped below the horizon, casting long shadows over the Holy City, Maya finished her shift at the community center. She waved goodbye to her colleagues, her mind already on the evening she planned to spend with Darius and his mother. The streets were bustling with activity, the sounds of the city a comforting backdrop as she made her way home.

Maya walked with a purposeful stride, her curly hair bouncing with each step. She was lost in thought, thinking about the stories Mrs. Thompson had shared and the warmth of their family dinners. The air was cool and crisp, a gentle breeze rustling the leaves of the trees lining the sidewalk.

As she turned down a quieter street, the atmosphere shifted. The sounds of the city seemed to fade, replaced by an eerie silence. Maya's instincts kicked in, and she quickened her pace, her eyes scanning her surroundings. She was only a few blocks from home, but the sense of unease grew stronger with each step.

Suddenly, a dark figure emerged from the shadows, blocking her path. Maya's heart raced as she recognized Malik "Shade" Thompson, his dark eyes gleaming with malice. Before she could react, two of his henchmen grabbed her from behind, their grips like iron.

"Well, well, what do we have here?" Malik said, his voice dripping with contempt. "Darius's little girlfriend. How convenient."

Maya struggled against the henchmen, her heart pounding in her chest. "Let me go!" she demanded, her voice steady despite the fear coursing through her veins.

Malik laughed, a cold, mocking sound that sent shivers down her spine. "Oh, I don't think so. You're coming with us. Darius will do anything to get you back, and that's exactly what I need."

With a swift motion, Malik signaled to his henchmen, and they dragged Maya into a waiting van. She fought with all her strength, but their grips were unyielding. The door slammed shut, and the van sped off into the night, leaving the quiet street behind.

Meanwhile, Darius was at home with his mother, enjoying a rare moment of peace. They were sitting in the living room, the soft glow of the lamp casting a warm light over the room. Mrs. Thompson was knitting, her hands moving with practiced ease, while Darius was lost in thought, his mind on the recent battles with Malik.

Suddenly, his phone buzzed. It was a message from Maya: "Help. Malik has me."

Darius's heart stopped. He read the message again, his mind racing. "Mom, I have to go," he said urgently, standing up and grabbing his jacket.

Mrs. Thompson looked up, her eyes filled with concern. "What's wrong, Darius?"

"It's Maya. Malik has her," Darius said, his voice tight with fear and anger. "I have to find her."

Mrs. Thompson stood up, her expression serious. "Be careful, Darius. And bring her back safe."

Darius nodded, his jaw set with determination. "I will, Mom. I promise."

Darius raced out of the apartment, his mind focused on one thing: finding Maya. He knew that Malik would use her to get to him, and he couldn't let that happen. He moved through the darkened streets with blinding speed, his enhanced senses guiding him.

He reached out to Marcus and Dr. Carter, explaining the situation and asking for their help. They quickly mobilized, using their resources to track down any leads on Malik's whereabouts. The community rallied around Darius, their support a beacon of hope in the darkness.

As the night wore on, Darius received a tip from one of Marcus's contacts. Malik was hiding out in an abandoned warehouse on the outskirts of the city. Darius didn't waste any time. He made his way to the warehouse, his heart pounding with a mix of fear and determination.

When he arrived, the warehouse was dark and foreboding, its windows shattered and its walls covered in graffiti. Darius moved cautiously, his senses on high alert. He could hear the faint sounds of voices inside, and he knew that Malik was waiting for him.

He burst through the door, his presence commanding attention. "Malik! Let her go!" he shouted, his voice echoing through the empty space.

Malik stepped forward, a dark smile playing on his lips. "Ah, Darius. Right on time. I knew you'd come."

Maya was tied to a chair in the center of the room, her eyes wide with fear but filled with determination. "Darius, be careful!" she called out, her voice steady despite the situation.

Darius's eyes blazed with anger. "This ends now, Malik. Let her go, and face me."

Malik laughed, a cold, mocking sound. "Oh, Darius, always the hero. But this time, you're outmatched."

Without warning, Malik launched himself at Darius, his movements a blur of speed and shadow. Darius barely had time to react, his enhanced senses allowing him to dodge Malik's initial attack. The two clashed in a violent explosion of energy, their powers colliding in a dazzling display of light and dark.

Malik cloaked himself in darkness, becoming nearly invisible as he moved. He used the shadows to create solid constructs, forming weapons that he wielded with deadly precision.

Malik phased through solid objects, making it nearly impossible for Darius to land a hit. He moved through walls and obstacles with ease, his form flickering like a ghost.

Malik unleashed powerful blasts of dark energy, the force of which sent shockwaves through the air. The energy crackled with malevolence, weakening and disorienting Darius with each hit.

Darius moved with incredible speed and grace, his punches and kicks landing with superhuman force. He leaped great distances, using his agility to evade Malik's attacks.

Darius's senses were razor-sharp, allowing him to anticipate Malik's moves and react with lightning speed. He could hear the faintest sounds and see in the dimmest light, giving him an edge in the dark.

Darius channeled his inner energy, creating protective barriers and unleashing powerful blasts of light. The energy crackled around him, a beacon of hope against Malik's darkness.

The fight was fierce and relentless, the two combatants moving with blinding speed. Malik's shadow constructs clashed with Darius's energy barriers, the impact sending sparks flying. The warehouse around them was torn apart, the ground cracking and splintering under the force of their blows.

Malik phased through a wall, reappearing behind Darius and striking with a shadowy blade. Darius spun around, his enhanced reflexes allowing him to block the attack just in time. He countered with a powerful punch, the force of which sent Malik sprawling.

Malik was relentless. He unleashed a barrage of dark energy blasts, each one hitting Darius with bone-jarring force. Darius staggered, his vision blurring as the energy sapped his strength. He knew he couldn't keep this up for long.

Malik's eyes gleamed with triumph as he saw Darius falter. "You're weak, Darius," he taunted. "You can't protect them all. You can't even protect yourself."

Darius gritted his teeth, his anger fueling his determination. He channeled his remaining energy, creating a blinding flash of light that momentarily disoriented Malik. Seizing the opportunity, Darius launched himself at Malik, landing a series of powerful blows.

But Malik recovered quickly, his intangibility allowing him to slip through Darius's grasp. He reappeared behind Darius, delivering a devastating blast of dark energy that sent Darius crashing to the ground.

Darius lay on the ground, his body battered and bruised. He knew he couldn't win this fight, not tonight. Summoning the last of his strength, he created a blinding flash of light, using it as a distraction to make his escape.

He staggered to his feet, his vision swimming as he stumbled towards Maya. He could hear Malik's mocking laughter echoing behind him, but he forced himself to keep moving. He had to get Maya out of there.

With a final burst of energy, Darius reached Maya and untied her. "We have to go," he said urgently, his voice tight with pain.

Maya nodded, her eyes filled with concern. "I'm right behind you."

They made their way out of the warehouse, Darius's strength waning with each step. But he knew he couldn't stop. He had to get Maya to safety.

As they emerged into the cool night air, Darius felt a surge of relief. They had escaped, but the battle was far from over. He knew that Malik would come after them again, and he had to be ready.

Maya looked at him, her eyes filled with gratitude and love. "Thank you, Darius. You saved me."

Darius smiled weakly, his heart swelling with emotion. "I promised I'd always come back to you."

They made their way back to the Thompson household, where Mrs. Thompson was waiting anxiously. She rushed to embrace them, her eyes filled with tears of relief.

"Thank God you're both safe," she said, her voice trembling with emotion.

Darius nodded, his resolve stronger than ever. "We're safe for now. But this isn't over.

The days following Maya's kidnapping were a whirlwind of chaos and fear. Malik "Shade" Thompson had intensified his assault on the city of Chicago, leaving the police stunned and powerless. The city was gripped by a sense of dread as Malik's attacks grew bolder and more destructive. The police held press conferences, vowing to bring the perpetrator to justice, but their words rang hollow in the face of Malik's relentless onslaught.

One evening, as Darius was patrolling the streets, he received a frantic call from Marcus. "Darius, it's your mother. Malik's men have taken her."

Darius's heart stopped. "Where is she?" he demanded, his voice tight with fear and anger.

"They've taken her to an old industrial facility on the outskirts of the city," Marcus said. "They're planning to blow it up with her inside."

Darius felt a surge of rage. He couldn't let Malik hurt his mother. "I'm on my way," he said, his voice filled with determination.

Darius raced to the facility, his mind focused on one thing: saving his mother. The building was a sprawling complex of rusted metal and crumbling concrete, its windows shattered and its walls covered in graffiti. He moved cautiously, his senses on high alert.

As he approached, he heard the sounds of struggle coming from inside. He burst through the door, his presence commanding attention. Malik's henchmen turned to face him, their expressions shifting from surprise to anger.

"Get out of my way," Darius growled, his eyes blazing with fury.

The henchmen lunged at him, but Darius was ready. He moved with blinding speed, his enhanced strength and agility allowing him to take them down one by one. He dodged their attacks with ease, his punches and kicks landing with superhuman force. The air crackled with energy as he unleashed powerful blasts of light, sending his enemies sprawling.

As Darius fought his way through the henchmen, he finally reached the room where his mother was being held. She was tied to a chair, her face bruised but her eyes filled with determination.

"Mom!" Darius cried, rushing to her side. "I'm here. I'm going to get you out of here."

Mrs. Thompson looked up at him, her eyes filled with love and relief. "Darius, be careful. Malik is here."

Just as Darius began to untie her, he heard a familiar, chilling voice. "Ah, Darius. Right on time."

He turned to see Malik standing in the doorway, his dark eyes gleaming with malice. "You really think you can save her? You're too late."

Without warning, Malik launched himself at Darius, his movements a blur of speed and shadow. Darius barely had time to react, his enhanced senses allowing him to dodge Malik's initial attack. The two clashed in a violent explosion of energy, their powers colliding in a dazzling display of light and dark.

Malik cloaked himself in darkness, becoming nearly invisible as he moved. He used the shadows to create solid constructs, forming weapons that he wielded with deadly precision.

Malik phased through solid objects, making it nearly impossible for Darius to land a hit. He moved through walls and obstacles with ease, his form flickering like a ghost.

Malik unleashed powerful blasts of dark energy, the force of which sent shockwaves through the air. The energy crackled with malevolence, weakening and disorienting Darius with each hit.

Darius moved with incredible speed and grace, his punches and kicks landing with superhuman force. He leaped great distances, using his agility to evade Malik's attacks.

Darius's senses were razor-sharp, allowing him to anticipate Malik's moves and react lightning speed. He could hear the faintest sounds and see in the dimmest light, giving edge in the dark.

Darius channeled his inner energy, creating protective barriers and unleashing powerful blasts of light. The energy crackled around him, a beacon of hope against Malik's darkness.

The fight was fierce and relentless, the two combatants moving with blinding speed. Malik's shadow constructs clashed with Darius's energy barriers, the impact sending sparks flying. The room around them was torn apart, the ground cracking and splintering under the force of their blows.

Malik phased through a wall, reappearing behind Darius and striking with a shadowy blade. Darius spun around, his enhanced reflexes allowing him to block the attack just in time. He countered with a powerful punch, the force of which sent Malik sprawling.

But Malik was relentless. He unleashed a barrage of dark energy blasts, each one hitting Darius with bone-jarring force. Darius staggered, his vision blurring as the energy sapped his strength. He knew he couldn't keep this up for long.

Malik's eyes gleamed with triumph as he saw Darius falter. "You're weak, Darius," he taunted. "You can't protect them all. You can't even protect yourself."

Darius gritted his teeth, his anger fueling his determination. He channeled his remaining energy, creating a blinding flash of light that momentarily disoriented Malik. Seizing the opportunity, Darius launched himself at Malik, landing a series of powerful blows.

But Malik recovered quickly, his intangibility allowing him to slip through Darius's grasp. He reappeared behind Darius, delivering a devastating blast of dark energy that sent Darius crashing to the ground.

Darius lay on the ground, his body battered and bruised. He knew he couldn't win this fight through sheer force alone. Summoning the last of his strength, he focused his energy, creating a protective barrier around himself and his mother.

Malik laughed, a cold, mocking sound. "You really think you can stop me, Darius? You're just one man."

Darius's eyes blazed with determination. "I'm not alone. I have the strength of my family, my friends, and my community behind me. And I won't let you win."

With a surge of energy, Darius broke through Malik's defenses, his punches and kicks landing with renewed force. The room shook with the impact of their blows, the air crackling with energy. Darius's determination fueled his strength, and he fought with everything he had.

In a final, desperate move, Darius channeled all his energy into one powerful blast of light. The force of it sent Malik sprawling, his dark energy dissipating into the air. Malik lay on the ground, defeated, his eyes filled with a mix of anger and disbelief.

"It's over, Malik," Darius said, his voice steady. "The city is safe, and you won't hurt anyone else."

Malik struggled to his feet, his expression one of rage. "This isn't over, Darius. I'll be back."

Darius shook his head, his eyes filled with resolve. "No, you won't. This ends now."

With that, Darius delivered a final, powerful blow, knocking Malik unconscious. The room fell silent, the air heavy with the aftermath of the battle.

Darius quickly untied his mother, his heart swelling with relief as he saw that she was safe. "Mom, are you okay?" he asked, his voice filled with concern.

Mrs. Thompson nodded, her eyes filled with love and pride. "I'm fine, Darius. You did it. You saved us."

Darius smiled, his heart full. "Let's get out of here."

They made their way out of the facility, the cool night air a welcome relief. The city was safe, and Malik's reign of terror was over. As they walked, Darius felt a sense of peace and fulfillment. He had protected his family, his community, and his city.

In the days that followed, the city of Chicago began to heal. The police, now empowered by Darius's victory, worked tirelessly to restore order and bring Malik's remaining henchmen to justice. Press conferences were held, and the city celebrated the end of Malik's reign of terror.

Darius, with the support of his mother and Maya, continued to protect the Holy City. He knew that there would always be challenges, but he was ready to face them with courage and determination. The bond between him and his community grew stronger, and life in the Holy City returned to normal.

As the sun set over the city, casting a warm, golden glow, Darius stood on the rooftop of his apartment building, looking out over the skyline. He felt a deep sense of gratitude and purpose. The battle between light and dark was far from over, but he knew that with the love and support of his family and friends, he could face whatever challenges lay ahead.

The Holy City was his home, and he would protect it with everything he had. And as the city held its breath, waiting for the next move, Darius stood ready, a beacon of hope in the darkness.